Steve's story is a remarkable on
take risks, to focus on discipleship, and to give God His
due glory. I am glad to call him a friend.

—ED STETZER
MISSIOLOGIST AND PRESIDENT OF
LIFEWAY RESEARCH
NASHVILLE, TN

Steve Murrell is clearly a leader who understands discipleship and who has been able to build it into the core
of his thriving church in the Philippines. There is much
to learn here. Steve's thoughts and principles are transferrable to every culture and generation. This is a much-
needed book for the church today. I highly recommend it!

—MARK CONNER
SENIOR PASTOR, CITYLIFE CHURCH
MELBOURNE, AUSTRALIA

The story of the growth of Victory, especially in the Philippines, is a tribute to Steve Murrell. He chose to follow
the footsteps of Jesus and focus on making disciples and
teams rather than building institutions. His book tells
the secret of their success and the story of Victory that is
so contagious and inspiring. The church worldwide can
learn from this well-written story—not just its methodology but also its underlying theology. A must-read for
every Christian leader.

—DR. JUN VENCER
GLOBAL TRANSFORMATION MINISTRIES, INC.
COLORADO SPRINGS, CO

Whether we are chosen accidentally or not, we have a mission: to make disciples of all nations. I salute the "same ole
boring strokes" because my life has never been the same
since I was discipled and started making disciples.

—"MARK," IRAN*

At long last, a true story that makes the extraordinary ordinary, the mystical practical, and the improbable possible. One comes away from this book saying, "I can do this. Let's encourage others to do this. Let's do this together." Our response to this has the potential to shake our world and shape the nations.

—Norman Nakanishi
Senior pastor, Grace Bible Church Pearlside
Pearl City, Hawaii

The first time I heard Steve was at a pastors' training school. The first speaker was a Babe Ruth kind of guy who told many testimonies of his spiritual home runs. I was amazed, inspired, and…discouraged. I thought, "This guy is awesome, but I could never be like him."

The next speaker, Steve, was not an evangelist, but he told many stories about ordinary people like myself who were trained to reach those around them. They were equipped by ordinary teachers to learn to share their faith in ordinary ways in ordinary places. He even exclaimed that he was not very good at it himself but had produced some success. Actually, this was an understatement. It was the success of those whom he had trained that caught my eye, and this was transferrable. Thanks, Steve, and thanks to our Filipino friends who dared to believe that anyone can reach the nations.

—Mike Watkins
Church planter, Kiev, Ukraine

Steve Murrell, through the experiences and realities written in this book, has made it crystal clear that all of us can do our part in fulfilling Jesus's command to "go and make disciples of all nations."

—Rouel Asuncion
Church planter, Dubai, United Arab Emirates

I have known Steve and Deborah Murrell for more than twenty-three years. I remember when they told me they were shifting to cell groups—do or die, no turning back. He and Deborah said they would start and not quit no matter how slow, or how costly, it became. Now thousands are involved in cell groups, and many cell groups have become twenty-first-century churches. We recommend you read this book and then say, "God, what You have done for this young leader, You can do with me." Believe it, pray it, and then go.

—Dr. Emanuele Cannistraci
Gateway City Church
San Jose, CA

I've had the privilege of knowing Steve Murrell since 1988. I've seen how the church has expanded from one place to many nations with his focus on discipleship unchanged. He trusted many insignificant people with the ministry and guided them to carry on. My testimony is just one of the examples of many. Honoring God and making disciples is the ultimate way to advance the kingdom of God.

—"Rocky," Bangladesh*

Reading Steve Murrell's book on discipleship makes me wish I was young again and had been taught these principles and practices. May the Lord richly bless this book to challenge today's church generation to rise and fulfill the Lord's original call!

—Kevin J. Conner
Author, *The Foundation of Christian Doctrine*
Melbourne, Australia

I am not an accidental missionary like Steve Murrell, but I became one of the hundreds of Filipino cross-cultural missionaries because the call to make disciples—not just in the Philippines but also in all nations—was inculcated in my heart and mind from the first day I became a Christian. I'm thankful to Steve because he has been faithful in reminding us again and again and again the same command Jesus gave in Matthew 28:19–20 to go and make disciples of all nations.

—"Mike," Vietnam*

The heartbeat of God is to see every soul won for His kingdom, every tribe redeemed, and every nation discipled. I recommend this book to be a handbook to all who desire to walk in the footsteps of Jesus.

—Shodankeh Johnson
Evangelical Fellowship of Sierra Leone
Freetown, Sierra Leone

Being born and raised in China, I had never heard about Jesus until the missionaries of Victory–Philippines walked onto my campus eleven years ago. I am glad they didn't just leave after I got saved but discipled me for four years. Now I am following their example in making disciples, and I have had the privilege of seeing many lives transformed.

—"Jackie," China*

WikiChurch is the life story of Steve Murrell, who had an ordinary beginning to the mission field that many of us can easily identify with regardless of our different personal, cultural, and language backgrounds. There is so much to emulate about his simple and sincere obedience to the Great Commission of Christ itself and his humble submission to leadership for the sake of it.

—Dr. John Thang
Senior pastor, Every Nation Church, Myanmar

Steve Murrell is an inspiration. His message is clear. His faith is authentic, and his thinking, strategic. God is using him to inspire the church to embrace the adventure of making a difference—by making disciples. The principles he lives by are both uncomplicated and life giving—but the challenge he brings is one that can't be ignored.

—Wayne Alcorn
Senior pastor, City Church
Queensland, Australia

Steve Murrell models for leadership around the world a true commitment to Christ. This book, *WikiChurch*, provides leaders of the ever-growing church the true biblical model of discipleship and church growth. A must book for all Christian leaders to read.

—Mel C. Mullen
Founding pastor, Word of Life Church Red Deer
Alberta, Canada

Steve Murrell is gifted when it comes to simplifying a process or concept. He always makes it so clear, precise, and practical! That's how discipleship should be. It's not some deep theology but achievable steps and processes that equip everyone to do it. To me, Steve exactly teaches and exemplifies discipleship.

—Timothy Loh
Senior pastor, Eaglepoint
Kuala Lumpur, Malaysia

* Name withheld for security purposes

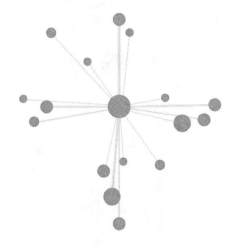

WIKICHURCH

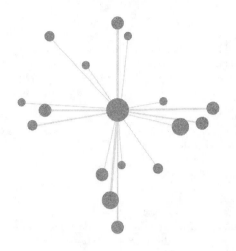

WIKICHURCH

Steve Murrell

CHARISMA
HOUSE

Most CHARISMA HOUSE BOOK GROUP products are available at special quantity discounts for bulk purchase for sales promotions, premiums, fundraising, and educational needs. For details, write Charisma House Book Group, 600 Rinehart Road, Lake Mary, Florida 32746, or telephone (407) 333-0600.

WIKICHURCH by Steve Murrell
Published by Charisma House
Charisma Media/Charisma House Book Group
600 Rinehart Road
Lake Mary, Florida 32746
www.charismahouse.com

Unless otherwise noted, all Scripture quotations are from the Holy Bible, New International Version. Copyright © 1973, 1978, 1984, International Bible Society. Used by permission.

Scripture quotations marked NAS are from the New American Standard Bible. Copyright © 1960, 1962, 1963, 1968, 1971, 1972, 1973, 1975, 1977, 1995 by the Lockman Foundation. Used by permission. (www.Lockman.org)

Scripture quotations marked NLT are from the Holy Bible, New Living Translation, copyright © 1996. Used by permission of Tyndale House Publishers, Inc., Wheaton, IL 60189. All rights reserved.

Visit the author's website at www.stevemurrell.com.
Follow him on Twitter at twitter.com/smurrell.

Library of Congress Cataloging-in-Publication Data:
Murrell, Steve.
  WikiChurch / Steve Murrell.
    p. cm.
  Includes bibliographical references (p.   ).
  ISBN 978-1-61638-444-9 (trade paper) -- ISBN 978-1-61638-428-9 (e-book)
  1. Discipling (Christianity) 2. Victory Christian Fellowship. 3. Murrell, Steve I. Title.
  BV4520.M84 2011
  253--dc22
                                          2011012333
11 12 13 14 15 — 9 8 7 6 5 4 3 2 1
Printed in the United States of America

To the Victory leadership team:
We all know that the ideas in this
book are ours, not mine.

To the Victory small group leaders:
I am challenged by the way you live to
honor God and make disciples.

ACKNOWLEDGMENTS

Whatever I know about discipleship and whatever I have accomplished in ministry, I owe a debt of gratitude to many people, especially these:

- Luther Mancao—the man who convinced me (and the Victory team) to transition from an event-based church to a small group discipleship–based church. Thanks for being so passionate about small group discipleship.

- Bishop Manny Carlos and Bishop Juray Mora—the men who now lead the Victory team. Thanks for your wisdom, integrity, faith, and, most of all, your friendship.

- Dr. Jun Escosar—one of the 1984 original members and now Victory's resident missiologist. Thanks for always reminding us that we are supposed to go and make disciples in every nation, not just the Philippines.

- Ferdie Cabiling—another 1984 original. Thanks for always keeping Victory small groups focused on reaching the lost.

- Joey Bonifacio—my longtime next-door neighbor and copastor. Thanks for your friendship and for all your creative discipleship ideas. Discipleship really is relationship.

- Ron Musselman—the Presbyterian youth pastor who engaged my world and established biblical foundations in my life. Thanks for preaching the gospel to me in 1975 and for teaching me how to follow Christ.

- Walter Walker—the campus missionary who equipped and empowered me to be a minister of the gospel and who helped turn these "same ole boring strokes" into a not-so-boring book. Thanks for giving me a chance to do ministry in 1981, and thanks for believing in and guiding this project.

- William, James, and Jonathan Murrell—three of my favorite people in the world. Thanks for living what I preach. Your lives inspire me to make disciples and honor God every day.

- Deborah Murrell—absolutely the best small group leader (and best friend) I have ever known. Thanks for saying yes to me in 1982 and for saying yes to God every day since then.

CONTENTS

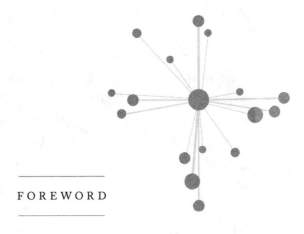

FOREWORD

I FIRST MET STEVE Murrell when he was a freshman and I was a junior at Mississippi State University. Although this was a few years before the film *Back to the Future* came out, I often tell people that Steve looked like Michael J. Fox's character in that popular 1985 movie. I have that memory association primarily because the insulated vest Steve wore that day was similar to the one Fox later wore in the movie. It looked like an overinflated life preserver. Maybe that image is so fixed in my mind because, since the day we met in 1978, Steve has been a kind of life preserver for me.

In 1978 I was struggling deeply with my newfound faith in Christ and had few friends who were bona fide Christians. I was beginning to sink a bit in the face of mounting fears about my new direction and pressures to return to my old lifestyle. Then, while I was sitting in a campus restaurant, in walked Steve Murrell. After striking up a conversation with me, he invited me to a campus fellowship meeting. That night my life would change forever. Among that small group of dedicated Christians I came to understand the call to follow Jesus, a call I would later embrace as the passion of my life.

Some of my fondest memories are of times when I was riding around with Steve in his car listening to Christian music. Steve was a man of few words back then, but the ones he spoke were usually golden. Having met Steve when he was already a committed Christian, it was hard for me to imagine him being the wild character he claimed to be before he met Jesus. He had also been an athlete with blazing speed, timing under ten seconds in the hundred-yard dash. Although fast and furious physically, inside Steve was a slow and steady plodder—the most consistent, methodical, and dependable person I have ever met.

When Steve accompanied me on that fateful mission trip to the Philippines in 1984, I had no idea that he would be God's choice to lead what would become one of the world's largest and finest churches. Nor did anyone else entertain those expectations, including Steve. Yet that is exactly what happened. It did not, however, happen suddenly, and it did not happen with great fanfare. The church grew from 165 to more than 52,000 in a manner that reflected Steve's leadership—through a consistent focus, methodical process, and dependable team. As Steve likes to say, the growth came after years of practicing the "same ole boring strokes."

He shares those "boring strokes" in this book, and the most encouraging part is that the discipleship principles actually work. In light of all the twenty-first-century innovation and gimmickry, the first-century strategy remains surprisingly relevant and effective. And Steve Murrell is one of the few pastors who have been patient and consistent enough to prove it. This success story, however, has not come about without its struggles. Having traveled to the Philippines countless times since 1984, I have seen Steve pay a high price to remain intently focused on making disciples. He has consistently resisted opportunities to divert from this course and adopt a more conventional, event-based ministry. Big meetings certainly look better in newsletters than small groups aimed at engaging nonbelievers for Christ.

Looking back, I think Steve probably decided early on that whatever he did in ministry and whatever success he attained, he would not direct the focus toward himself. He has never seemed to care about being the big conference speaker but has been content to simply make disciples and equip and empower them to make other disciples. That lack of pretense permeates the ministry in the Philippines and the rest of the Every Nation family of churches for which Steve serves as president.

Anyone who has traveled overseas knows the caricature of the "ugly American"—the visitor from the United States who is loud, brash, and thinks he knows it all. Unfortunately, that is the image many Christian leaders project when they travel to the Philippines. These ministers see the warmth and generosity of the Filipino people and do all they can to take advantage of them—to be served by them instead of being their servant. I think Steve vowed to single-handedly break that stereotype. One of the few times I have seen Steve Murrell upset was at a conference he hosted in Manila. The front row of seats had been occupied almost entirely by white-faced Americans. Just as Jesus did when He took the whip and cleared the temple, Steve quickly made sure that the visitors were all ushered to seats further back so the locals could fill the places of honor.

Rather than trying to establish, protect, or promote his position, Steve has been trying to work himself out of a job since the day he landed in Manila. He constantly encourages, trains, and empowers others to lead. The fruit of that philosophy shines brightly in the grateful attitudes and fierce loyalty among the leaders with whom Steve has served through the years. That core group of men and women has stood together in tight unity for nearly three decades and has produced something that truly brings honor to God. It's ironic that a city with legendary smog and pollution has some of the cleanest "spiritual air" you can breathe. Attending a Victory conference, you cannot help but be impacted by such a powerful sense of purity, unity, and undistracted devotion to Christ. Victory–Manila has exported that same contagious spirit as it has planted new churches throughout Asia.

I have known Steve long enough and well enough to understand that he could write thick volumes about the principles and applications for making disciples. No one I know has thought about discipleship, practiced it, refined it, and succeeded at it more than he. Yet in keeping with his own style, his own life's objective, and his own way of leading others, he makes his big point in a clear, concise, and compelling way: go and make disciples!

Having known him all these years, I can attest that he is no super saint. He is simply a man who reads his Bible, loves his family, and continues to show up day in and day out. His family and friends have grown to lean heavily on that dependability. It's the kind of steady hand that is desperately needed in today's turbulent climate.

Next to his relationship with God and certainly before his ministry duties comes Steve's family. I met his wife, Deborah, while she was a student at the University of Georgia. Although she was a popular student and a member of a sorority on campus, she was a committed believer and a bold witness. It was no surprise that these two people would find each other and change the world as they have. Their commitment to each other has allowed them to weather the storms that would have taken out most.

It's been quite a journey since Steve and I first walked around a two-thousand-seat auditorium in Manila in 1984, dreaming of the day we would be able to fill it. It would have never entered our minds to believe for the tens of thousands who are now an active part of the ministry. Many try to dismiss the growth of churches in Asia as compared to the stagnation of American churches. But as Steve points out in this book, the phenomenal growth of Victory–Manila has been in the midst of overall church decline in their nation. The reason Victory–Manila has grown when others have not is primarily because they have sold out to making disciples. After reading this book, I'm sure you will be ready to sell out too.

Steve says it best when he says, "Jesus told us to make disciples and that He would build the church. Instead, we try to build the church and continue to neglect making disciples." His words are like that life preserver I described in the beginning. The principles outlined in this book are being offered to a struggling, drowning church in the West. If we will reach out and embrace those principles, it could prove to be the very lifeline that rescues us from frustration and futility, returning us to the fruitfulness that the Bible promises.

—Rice Broocks

Rice Broocks is the cofounder of the Every Nation Ministries, which has established churches and campuses in more than seventy nations. He is also the senior minister of Bethel World Outreach Church, a multisite, multigenerational, and multiethnic church based in Nashville, Tennessee. He has a master's degree from Reformed Theological Seminary and a doctorate in missiology from Fuller Theological Seminary. He currently resides in Franklin, Tennessee, with his wife, Jody, and their five children.

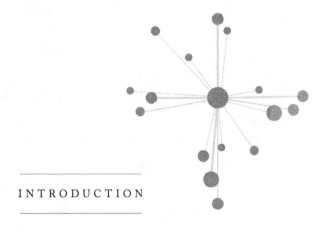

WHAT IS A WIKICHURCH?

I LOOKED AROUND AND silently wondered, "Who are all these people, and where did they come from?" After waiting in line for hours, thousands of energetic Filipinos were packed into the iconic Araneta Coliseum, the largest domed arena in the Philippines. Also known as the Big Dome, the arena was the site of the "Thrilla in Manila," the legendary 1975 fight between boxing champs Muhammad Ali and Joe Frazier. But on this Sunday in August 2009, the crowd wasn't gathered for a boxing match but for the twenty-fifth anniversary of a church called Victory, the congregation my wife and I helped start in 1984.

Deborah and I originally planned to be in Manila for one month, but we stayed a bit longer, and at some point in time we became "accidental missionaries." I looked up to the nose-bleed section—scanning the left, the right, the back—and couldn't help but thank God for giving me the privilege of serving the Filipino people for more than half my life.

As the band cranked out upbeat worship songs, the crowd enthusiastically expressed their love to God in that unique Filipino way. The worship was followed by a history video, powerful testimonies, and hip-hop dance complete with laser lights and high-tech holograms. Because Filipinos love to laugh, we even had some comedy routines in the mix before I preached a short anniversary sermon.

Then that group filed out, and thousands more who were already waiting outside squeezed in so we could do the same routine all over again. Despite having multiple services, another thirteen thousand Victory members who did not get their tickets quickly enough had to watch the service live over the Internet or wait for the podcast.

Who are all these people, and where did they come from? It was actually a rhetorical question. Of course I knew where they came from—from our eighty-one weekend worship services held in fifteen Victory locations across metro Manila. A few pastors and campus missionaries had also come in from the forty-five Victory churches that we planted throughout the Philippine Islands. Even some of our Filipino cross-cultural missionaries had flown in from Thailand, Bangladesh, China, Dubai, and other locations I cannot list because of our security protocols.

Most of the people were under the age of thirty. All were serious Christ-followers, dedicated to honoring God and making disciples. More than thirty-five hundred of them led weekly discipleship groups in coffee shops, dorm rooms, living rooms, and boardrooms all over the metro area.

After scanning the rafters, I looked at the first few rows—at the pastors, their wives, and their kids. Good memories flooded my mind. Years ago I had baptized many of these men and women, officiated at their weddings, and dedicated their kids. I have worked with some of them for twenty-five years. Others have been around for only a few years but are nevertheless a vital part of the team.

Most of the people in the Big Dome that day were a lot younger than me, and most were relatively poor—at least compared to Western standards. The crowd was diverse, nonetheless. There were some elderly people in the coliseum as well as wealthy individuals, including an assortment of politicians, movie stars, rock stars, professional basketball players, and wannabe celebrities.

How did a guy from Jackson, Mississippi, with no missionary training and little financial support end up as the founder and leader of this group? More importantly, how did a small band of young Filipinos emerge from the poverty, riots, and political chaos of Manila's University Belt in the mid-1980s to become a significant influence in their country and in a dozen other nations? How all this happened is what this book is about.

When friends from abroad visit us, they often refer to our church as a miracle. I don't really think about it that way. We have not grown in size, depth, and influence as a result of revival meetings, supernatural manifestations, healing miracles, or celebrity endorsements. Sure, miracles do occur periodically, people encounter God's presence regularly, and every now and then a celebrity will decide to follow Christ. None of these, however, have anything to do with Victory's character, size, or "flywheel momentum."

If you were to suggest that Victory's growth was somehow driven by my personality and gifting, you would have a hard time convincing any Filipinos of that. I am probably the least evangelistic preacher and the least charismatic leader on our whole team. What has happened at Victory is not simply a miracle, and it is certainly not mass attraction to a spiritual superstar. To understand how we grew from 165 university students to more than 52,000 members you have to understand the concept of what I call a "WikiChurch" and the origins of Wikipedia.

WIKI WHAT?

Where do you go when you need information fast? Like millions around the world, I go straight to Wikipedia, the world's largest free online encyclopedia. The "wiki" part of Wikipedia is from a Hawaiian word meaning "quick." While it may seem as though Wikipedia has had quick success, it was actually a bit of an accident.

In 2000 Jimmy Wales and Larry Sanger started an online encyclopedia called Nupedia. The goal was for it to include contributions written only by experts. Before an article could be posted on Nupedia, it had to go through an extensive scholarly review process. That strategy proved to be painstakingly slow. When Nupedia unplugged its servers in 2003, only twenty-four articles had been posted, and seventy-four were in the review process.[1] There were not very many articles, but they were scholarly and professionally written!

Imagine if every believer, not just paid ministers, did ministry. That's a WikiChurch. That's the Book of Acts. That's Victory–Manila.

In 2001, one year after Nupedia launched, Wales and Sanger started Wikipedia as a feeder system for Nupedia. The idea was to allow non-pros, non-scholars, and non-experts to write articles that the Nupedia scholars would review. The articles would then make their way through the extensive Nupedia approval process. By the end of 2001, volunteers had submitted more than twenty thousand "wiki" articles.[2]

It took the experts three years to create twenty-four articles and the non-experts one year to create twenty thousand articles. At the time of this writing, contributors from around the world had submitted more than seventeen million Wikipedia articles, and according to an independent survey, most are as accurate as traditional encyclopedia entries written by recognized experts.[3]

Unfortunately, many churches today function more like Nupedia than Wikipedia. They allow only credentialed professionals to lead evangelism and discipleship efforts while volunteers are expected to show up and pay up, but not engage in serious ministry. Imagine if the situation were reversed. Imagine if every believer, not just paid leaders, were engaged in ministry. That's a WikiChurch. That's the Book of Acts. That's what is behind Victory–Manila's growth.

I love what Michael Scott, the fictional regional manager on the sitcom *The Office*, says about Wikipedia: "Wikipedia is the best thing ever. Anyone, in the world, can write anything they want about any subject. So you know you are getting the best possible information."[4]

Wikipedia may be an imperfect source, but it has made information widely available simply by empowering volunteers. That, I believe, is the call of the church—to empower imperfect people to spread the most important message around the world. Victory–Manila grew because we became a WikiChurch, and we became a WikiChurch not by bouncing from revival to revival or from strategy to strategy. We simply practiced the same ole boring strokes year after year.

SAME OLE BORING STROKES

All three of my sons played junior tennis in Asia and college tennis in the United States. Like most competitive tennis players, they benefited from multiple coaches at different stages in their development, but no one helped them as much as Coach Tom.

"Up, down, up. Topspin is your friend. Same ole boring strokes! Up, down, up. Up, down, up." Tom barked the same instructions every day, like a military drill sergeant preparing his troops for battle.

He was not much of a motivator, but Coach Tom knew proper tennis technique, and he was a master teacher who never strayed from the basics. "Up, down, up. Same ole boring strokes"—every day, over and over, like a broken record.

Tom would say, "You wanna win? Then you have to *master the same ole boring strokes*. Up, down, up. That's how you create topspin, and topspin is your friend. Nothing fancy. Same ole boring strokes!"

I think I lead the church the same way Tom coaches tennis. You want to make disciples? It doesn't require anything fancy. Just the same ole boring strokes: engage, establish, equip, empower. Engage, establish, equip, empower. Engage, establish, equip, empower. And that's about all we have been doing at Victory since 1984. The same ole boring strokes.

Like competitive young tennis hopefuls, church leaders all over the world tend to copy the latest programs and methods, hoping to discover that elusive secret key to church growth. However, rather than looking for a growth gimmick, our starting point has always been simple obedience to the Great Commission: "Therefore go and make disciples of all nations" (Matt. 28:19). We are not looking for a "silver bullet" solution. We are not swinging for the fence. We are not jacking up desperation half-court shots. We are just making disciples. Same ole boring strokes.

In the last twenty-seven years, all our efforts, all our mistakes, and all our successes have been in pursuit of figuring out how to make disciples. After all, if you do one thing consistently and focus on it exclusively, you cannot help but get better at it. Even a blind man will stumble upon the correct path if he keeps walking long enough.

Building a Church or Making Disciples?

Gradually we at Victory learned a few things, put those into practice, and evaluated the results. We threw out ideas that did not work, changed others to make them more effective, and have continued refining our discipleship process nonstop. The result has been that we initially went through a period of steady growth. Then we made some changes that turned into faster growth. Time will tell, but our latest adjustments seem to be producing multiplication.

In 2007, after my wife and I had been living in the Philippines for twenty-three years, my ministry responsibilities expanded to include helping churches around the world. As a result, we started splitting our time between Manila and Nashville, Tennessee, flying back and forth every couple of months. Every time I return to Manila, the church is larger, confirming what I have said since the beginning. It is not about me—never has been, never will be. It is not even about getting big. We have found that if we simply focus on making disciples who are equipped and empowered to make other disciples, then health, strength, and growth happen naturally.

If we simply focus on making disciples
who are equipped and empowered
to make other disciples, then health,
strength, and growth happen naturally.

Jesus told His followers that He would build His church. Then one of the last things He told them to do was make disciples. It's that simple. We make disciples, and He builds the church. We do not build the church, and He does not make disciples. All we've done at Victory–Manila since 1984 is to make disciples, and He continues to build those disciples into a church.

The Victory story is about a remarkable team of leaders who began together as teenagers. Over time we developed a simple, culturally relevant process of making disciples. Though we are still evaluating, refining, and constantly rewriting our discipleship materials, the underlying principles of the disciple-making process at Victory are firmly fixed. This book is partly about the discipleship process, but it is also about the importance of creating a *discipleship culture.*

My prayer is that when you finish reading these pages, you will be inspired to compassionately *engage* your community, intentionally *establish* biblical foundations, strategically *equip* believers, and constantly *empower* disciples. Basically, I hope you will discover how joining the WikiChurch movement will revolutionize your life, your church, and your world.

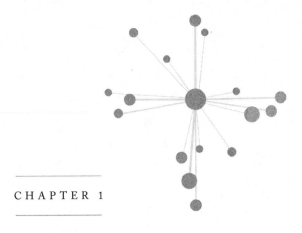

CHAPTER 1

THE
RELUCTANT LEADER

IT WAS ONE of the loneliest moments of my life. My wife, Deborah, and I watched the huge Philippine Airlines 747 taxi down the runway and head to Seoul, South Korea, with our entire team, leaving the two of us behind in a foreign city.

Loneliness when mixed with fear and insecurity can create a strange and powerfully destructive state of mind. It can bring all kinds of irrational thoughts, fears, and doubts. In our brief month in Manila we had already experienced some scary stuff, including gale-force typhoons, flash floods, student riots, tear gas, and strange food. We had also seen hundreds of Filipinos respond to the gospel. And now our team was leaving, and the two of us were staying in Manila, along with four other American volunteers.

I had a lot of questions and few answers. Why didn't we get on that plane with the rest of the Americans? Can we really do this by ourselves? How will we pay the bills?

This was supposed to be a two-month summer mission trip—one month in Manila, Philippines, followed by one month in Seoul, South Korea. But it looked like that one month in Manila was turning into our own personal *Groundhog Day*. Like in the 1993 film, it seemed that month would repeat itself indefinitely.

We would have to find a way to deal with our fears, feelings of inadequacy, and lack of funds. However, the bigger, more pressing issue was who would lead the young church now that the Americans were gone. There had been a leadership plan, but it was becoming more and more evident that the plan was not working. Someone had to stay behind to work on developing a permanent leadership team for the new church. Since no one else stepped up to the plate, Deborah and I said good-bye to the American team and stayed behind. That's why I call myself an accidental missionary.

I WOULD RATHER FOLLOW THAN LEAD

I'm a reluctant leader, a natural-born follower. Every leadership position in which I have found myself seems to have come upon me by default. Whenever the need arose for someone to take charge, everyone else seemed to be headed out of town. My life has been like a familiar old comedy routine. Troops are lined up, and volunteers are asked to step forward. Invariably, everyone steps backward while one person stands still. On several occasions I have been the guy with no particular ambition for a new assignment who naïvely stood his ground while everyone else slowly stepped backward.

It was never my intention to become a missionary or a leader. A summer in the Philippines had never occurred to my wife and me until I got a call from my friend Rice Broocks. Deborah and I were newlyweds focused on our little campus ministry at Mississippi State University (MSU), and Rice was recruiting a team of college students for summer outreaches in South Korea and the Philippines.

I had never met a Filipino and didn't know anything about the Philippines except that it is an island nation on the other side of the world. Rice was pretty excited about taking a team there. He is an extraordinarily persuasive person, especially when it comes to evangelism, campus ministry, and church planting. It was May 1984, and the departure date was only six weeks away. We would need five thousand dollars for the two-month trip—a fortune to us at the time. I told Rice, "Sounds good, but we don't have any money. I guess if God provides, then we'll go with you." God provided, and we went.

Thinking back on our decision, the reason Deborah and I made that two-month commitment was primarily to help an old friend. I can vaguely remember Rice's passionate appeal: "Steve, you've got to go. We need you and Deborah. I have this huge team, and I need someone to organize and train them." Anyway, there was not much going on during the summer in the sleepy little college town of Starkville, Mississippi. Rice had graduated from MSU and was traveling to campuses all over the United States preaching to students. We were still in Starkville because when the leader of our struggling campus fellowship moved to another college, we inherited the position.

In retrospect, our decision to go to Manila for the summer was more than someone else's need to recruit a team or the fact that we had nothing better to do. I had been recruited for good ideas before and have been hundreds of times since. Even without a good excuse, I typically have no hesitation to decline. Through the years I have become very good at saying no. Sometimes I even do it emphatically: "No!"

The decision to go was not based on any great revelation from God. I do not even recall praying about the request with Deborah. I suppose that somewhere deep inside there was some sense of being led by the Spirit, even if it was simply a divinely inspired perspective that made it seem like the right decision. I am all for being led by the Holy Spirit, but my clearest sense of calling is more like an ancient letter from God framed on the wall rather than the morning Twitter message about what is on His mind at the moment. The last command Jesus gave to His disciples was:

> Go and make disciples of all nations, baptizing them in the name of the Father and of the Son and of the Holy Spirit, and teaching them to obey everything I have commanded you. And surely I am with you always, to the very end of the age.
>
> —MATTHEW 28:19–20

Since we have not yet reached the end of the age, I have always assumed that He still wants us to go to the nations and make disciples, and that He is still with us.

The point is that there was no booming voice or even a still, small voice saying, "My son, I have called you to the mission field." Even though I did not really grow up in church, I have heard people talk about "receiving the call." It didn't happen that way for me, at least not at the beginning. I did not go to the Philippines because I received a specific calling from God. I just got a phone call from Rice. There was no divine mandate except Jesus's Great Commission to go and make disciples.

I guess I've always believed that God's calling is a "standing order" to go and make disciples. That mandate for every believer has been impressed on me since the day I surrendered my life to Christ. It was drilled into me first by Ron Musselman, the youth pastor at First Presbyterian Church in Jackson, Mississippi, then by Walter Walker, the campus missionary at Mississippi State University. So it was with that same sense of perpetual calling and commission to go and make disciples that I agreed to participate in the two-month summer mission trip to Manila and Seoul.

I've always believed that God's
calling is a "standing order"
to go and make disciples.

Tear Gas, Riot Police, and Summer Missions

When the team of sixty-five eager American summer missionaries landed in Manila in June 1984, the Philippines was in the middle of a national crisis, ablaze with student protests and riots that were quickly growing into a popular revolt. Manila in 1984 was much like the 2011 Egyptian revolt that ousted Hosni Mubarak. The event that ignited the wildfire was the August 1983 assassination of former Senator Benigno Aquino Jr. on the Manila International Airport tarmac as he returned from a three-year, self-imposed exile. Aquino was the iconic leader of the democratic struggle against President Ferdinand Marcos. Marcos had held onto dictatorial power with the help of martial law since 1972. (The Marcos regime was eventually overthrown without bloodshed during the 1986 People Power Revolution.)

Anti-government outrage sparked by Aquino's assassination was sweeping over the general populace. The economy was in a state of collapse as investors pulled money out of the Philippines to invest it in more stable countries. The erosion of capital even had begun to elicit protest from the usually passive business community. But nowhere was the revolt more intense than among students attending universities along C. M. Recto Avenue, known as Manila's University Belt, or simply U-Belt.

After meeting for two weeks at the Girl Scouts Auditorium near U-Belt, we leased the basement of the Tandem Cinema, a run-down movie theater located in the middle of the largest concentration of colleges and universities in the

Philippines. That basement could easily seat about two hundred fifty people, but if we packed everyone in sardine-style, we could squeeze in four hundred.

There was no air conditioning, no windows, and no fresh air to breathe. The smell was horrible. Sewer pipes from the cinema ran across the low ceiling. Some of them had been leaking for years. Tear gas occasionally drifted in from the Recto Avenue riots, adding to the unforgettable mix of aromas. It was like being on the bad end of the Deuteronomy 28 promise of blessings and curses. A massive cleanup effort made the room minimally bearable, but after starting off in a place like that, we had nowhere to go but up.

The U-Belt campuses that surrounded our facility were the places where leftist, communist, and anti-Marcos movements had gained footholds. Almost every day thousands of activist students with clenched fists and the standard red banners would march down Recto Avenue past the Tandem Cinema on their way to the presidential palace. At the barricades along the foot of Mendiola Bridge, the students confronted the army and the riot police. The tension in the confrontations increased each day.

We had been conducting evangelistic meetings daily, sometimes several times a day. Our drama team was out on the streets with their mime productions. (Before you laugh, remember we're talking about 1984.) Others would gather crowds on the campuses for preaching rallies. There were hundreds of one-to-one gospel presentations and invitations to our meetings. That summer we saw a lot of angry students shouting, chanting, and running from water cannons, riot police, and tear gas. But we were finding that behind that anger were open hearts hungry for God and ready for a change.

Culturally, Deborah and I were a long, long way from Starkville, Mississippi. If we had known the chaos we were getting into, we might have chosen a different summer mission trip—maybe to Jamaica, Europe, or Australia. But what looked like the worst of times turned out to be God's perfect timing. The Holy Spirit began to work in that situation, and by the time the outreach team left, we had the beginnings of a church with about 165 new Filipino believers. Most were poor students from the provinces; many were political protesters; some were radical leftist student leaders.

COMPELLED BY COMPASSION

For the first two weeks nightly meetings were held at the Girl Scouts Auditorium, but because the auditorium was not available on weekends, we held our Sunday morning worship services at the Admiral Hotel on Roxas Boulevard. It was in the Admiral Hotel function room on our third Sunday that we held our first Communion service in the Philippines. It was by far the most significant Communion service of my life. It would be hard to describe how tangibly we sensed the presence of the Holy Spirit in that meeting. We were all on our knees praying when something extraordinary happened. Though I am a rather stoic individual who was raised to think that real men do not cry, I have to admit that my eyes were sweating—well, gushing like broken water faucets might be a better description.

---

*Nothing has more
potential to complicate your life
than a clear calling from God.*

I have been a believer since I was sixteen years old and a pastor/preacher for thirty years. In all those years I can count only three times when God has spoken to me with undeniable clarity. The first time was a sense that Deborah was to be my wife. Fortunately, she agreed. The third time I "know that I know" God spoke to me was several years later. It had to do with the first church property we bought in Manila. I had no idea what was about to happen to the Philippine economy, but I just knew God said we were to avoid debt and pay cash. Soon afterward the Philippine peso crashed, and interest rates soared to 30 percent. Had we used debt to purchase that property, we would have been in big trouble.

That morning in Manila's Admiral Hotel was the second time I know I heard God's voice. Kneeling by my chair, the Holy Spirit was putting a supernatural compassion in my heart for the Filipino people that was greater than any vision or dream I could have conjured up on my own. It was as if God switched something on inside of me. The apostle Paul wrote to the Corinthian church, "Christ's love compels us" (2 Cor. 5:14). My involvement in the church that would become Victory–Manila was birthed in that moment, not out of a great vision or some sense of destiny. From the beginning we were motivated or "compelled" by compassion for lost people. Vision gradually grew out of that.

You might think that such a certain sense of God's calling

would answer many questions and clarify lots of details. That was not the case with us. Nothing has more potential to complicate your life than a clear calling from God. Before that Sunday morning, the plan was one month in Manila, one month in South Korea, and back to normal life in Mississippi. Now I knew that God wanted me to stay in the Philippines, but what did that mean—another month, a year, or the rest of my life?

I thought long and hard about how to present this to my wife. To the extent that my missionary career was accidental and my leadership reluctant, Deborah's was far more. She grew up in an Assemblies of God church and had prayed to marry a pastor, but now it looked as if that pastor was about to become a cross-cultural missionary. Living in Asia was not part of her plan. In time, as she gave her life to serve and disciple Filipino students, she became as convinced as I was that we were supposed to be in the Philippines.

LEADING
AND LEAVING

As the day of the American team's departure drew near, there was a growing concern about what to do with our fledgling student church. Rice and I had challenged the sixty-five American summer missionaries to reproduce themselves by discipling a Filipino new believer to fill their places. Unfortunately, there was no time for a lengthy training school. Because we saw ourselves as temporary missionaries, we had to quickly train Filipinos in basic ministry skills. In just a matter of weeks the Filipino converts would be the ones to pray with others to receive Christ, explain water baptism, pray for them to be filled with the Holy Spirit, and take them through basic spiritual foundations. We all felt the urgency to equip, empower, and get out of the way. This forced the team and the new Filipino believers to look to and trust in the Holy Spirit.

Because I scored close to zero for spiritual gifts related to evangelism, we began working as hard as we could to do what we could. For me, that meant discipling and teaching foundations to young Filipinos who had so decisively accepted Christ as Savior and Lord. Everything we did in that extra month in Manila was motivated by the concept I had heard over and over at the Mississippi State University campus ministry: work yourself out of a job. Years later someone commented on the scores of young leaders who continually emerge from Victory–Manila. They were wondering aloud why American churches by comparison produce so few. Deborah's response struck right at the heart of the matter. "From the very beginning," she said, "it was never about creating a position or a ministry for ourselves. We were always leading with the idea of leaving."

The second four weeks went by quickly. Then we flew to Seoul, South Korea, to meet up with the American team for the long flight home. Within two weeks of our return we were in Dallas, Texas, at a staff meeting with the leaders of the ministry with which we were associated. The question of leadership for the new church in the Philippines was on the agenda for discussion. Deborah and I stood in front of about one hundred twenty leaders to give a report about the young church, and we were subsequently grilled about what we felt the Lord had spoken to us. It was one of our first such staff meetings, and we did not give the answers that some wanted to hear. I learned later that the closed-door discussions went something like this: "Who is Steve Murrell, what has he done, and what makes us think he can be trusted to build a significant church in Manila?"

Apparently those concerns were too great for the senior ministry leaders to overlook. I couldn't help but wonder what was the meaning of that Admiral Hotel moment, that overwhelming sense of God's love for the Filipino people, and the undeniable calling to stay in Manila if we were not to be allowed to return to the Philippines. As I said earlier, a clear sense of God's calling does not necessarily make things simple. Through the years I've learned that God rarely speaks so loudly that everyone around you hears it too. We definitely felt God wanted us to return to help establish the church in Manila. However, because the leaders of our ministry did not approve of our plan, there was nothing for Deborah and me to do but to trust our future to the Lord.

We headed back to Starkville thinking the decision was made and the conversation was over. Not that the leadership issue in the Philippines was settled; in the brief time since our departure, the leadership need had become even more obvious. The discussion about our involvement was indeed over as far as we were concerned. Apparently I was not old enough, experienced enough, or anointed enough to be trusted with such an important assignment. The X factor, however, was my friend Rice Broocks. He was a part of that ongoing conversation among the senior leaders, and he believed I was the man for the job. Over and against the collective wisdom of that meeting, Rice had great faith in Deborah and me. Better said, he trusted in the power and grace of God to enable us. There is nothing like having someone in your corner with that kind of confidence. But that is quintessential Rice Broocks. He usually believes in people much more than they believe in themselves.

BETWEEN MISSISSIPPI AND MANILA

A couple of weeks after the Dallas staff meeting, I got another call from Rice. Apparently his faith in us had overcome everyone else's doubts. As soon as we hung up the phone, we were again packing our bags, this time for a six-month stint in Manila to help develop the leadership team, a team made up of new believers.

I have never forgotten what it was like to have someone believe in me, especially when others did not. You might say that I have never gotten over it. Back in Manila, we began training young Filipino leaders who had surrendered their lives to Jesus just a few months before. I was never quite sure about the extent of our calling to serve the Filipino people. That one-month mission trip turned into two because no one else volunteered to stay. Then, despite senior leadership concerns, it turned into six months. At the two-year mark, Deborah and I knew that we were to dig in for the long haul and commit ourselves to equipping and empowering a new generation of Filipino leaders. We have been in the Philippines now for twenty-seven years. A lot has happened since that first outreach in 1984. We've lived through seven coup attempts, a couple of People Power revolutions, a volcano, a few earthquakes, countless brownouts, floods, and annual typhoons. We've made lots of friends and recorded countless memories.

I have never forgotten what it was like to have someone believe in me, especially when others did not.

Quite honestly, the first few coups were a bit unnerving, but after a while we got used to them. The same with the typhoons. Deborah and I eventually learned to sleep though the hurricane-force winds, but I still remember nights with no power and three scared little boys crawling into our bed as our house shook and the winds howled.

I also vividly remember sitting in my "office" at a Dunkin' Donuts on Recto Avenue one hot July afternoon in 1984 trying to write a vision/mission/purpose statement for our new church. The first thing I scribbled on that DD napkin was: "We exist to honor God." The honor and glory of God would be our starting point and our finish line. Whether or not we grew to be a large church was never the point. It is still not about becoming big, and it is still not about me. It is about honoring God and making disciples.

Many people search for, pray for, and spend their lives preparing for a clear and definitive sense of God's calling and purpose for their lives. How they hunger for something so much bigger than themselves—that one thing for which they were created! Some want it so badly and seek it so hard that they are tempted to interpret the slightest inclination or circumstance as the call of God. Others go to such great ends in order to find it that they are tempted to manufacture it in their own minds. My experience tells me that if we are ever to find that special grace and calling, we will most likely find it while in pursuit of doing what God has already called us to do. For me, that meant embracing the Great Commission as my own. Following the Lord's command generally led me to a more specific understanding of what God wanted from my life. It is much like the rudder on a ship. If the ship is not moving at a minimum speed, the rudder is useless. You cannot be guided unless you are moving.

We exist to honor God.

The decision to stay in the Philippines did not mean that I considered myself prepared for it. I had no financial support, no time to properly raise a partnership team, and no training in cross-cultural missions. I was not a great evangelist (and still am not). I was not a dynamic speaker or an inspirational leader. My paltry leadership experience consisted of two years leading a campus group of thirty people at MSU. I was relatively young, unproven, and untrained. What I did not understand was the relative part. In other words, I was young, unproven, and untrained relative to or compared to normal church standards of leadership in America. Those things were not as important in the Philippines. In Manila, all I needed was to get busy doing what I knew how to do—making disciples and teaching the foundations of the Christian faith.

WikiChurch Lessons

I am an accidental missionary and a reluctant leader. I never set out or intended to be either one. I never intended to pastor a big church, never intended to be the leader of an international mission and church-planting organization. All I ever wanted to do was honor God and make disciples. That simple approach does not always make things easy; in fact, it can make things quite difficult at times. But it has simplified our lives. Honor God, make disciples—everything else has followed from that.

I was a clueless kid with virtually no missionary training and very little financial support. Yet I went from a struggling campus minister in Mississippi to serving as a cross-cultural church planter in Manila. God often chooses the unlikely candidates to carry out His plan, and He gave me the tools I needed. He even taught me some "spiritual judo." In fact, looking back it's clear that Victory's success is the result of our mastering just one unstoppable move.

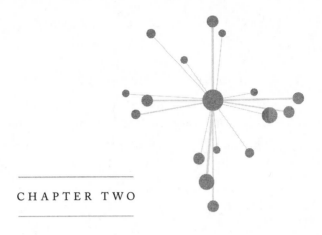

CHAPTER TWO

ONE-ARMED JUDO

T HERE ONCE WAS a judo master whose student was involved in a serious auto accident. The ten-year-old boy's left arm was so badly injured that it had to be amputated. Everyone thought that would end the boy's judo aspirations. However, the loss of an arm only increased the boy's determination to compete. So, despite the amputation, the judo master agreed to continue training the boy, but he focused all the training on one extremely difficult move. The boy complained, wanting to be just like the others who were learning all aspects of the sport. The old master convinced his one-armed student not to question but to learn. So they practiced that one move day after day, week after week, month after month.

Eventually the one-armed boy was allowed to enter a judo tournament where he surprised everyone by advancing through several rounds and into the finals. His opponent in the championship round was faster, stronger, and more experienced. This guy had mastered dozens of judo techniques. And he had two arms. The one-armed boy seemed completely outmatched. Spectators admired his courage and determination but felt sorry for him. Then at one point in the contest the superior athlete lost concentration. At that moment the one-armed boy executed his one move. There was nothing his opponent could do to escape. After the match everyone wanted to know how a one-armed boy could possibly be the champion.

"He won for two reasons," his teacher answered. "First of all, he has mastered one of the most difficult moves in all of judo. Second, the only defense against that move is to grab your opponent's left arm." I do not know if the story is true, but it has circulated around locker rooms and pulpits for years in various forms. It may be just motivational speaker legend, but it does make a good point about the importance of discipleship. The Victory–Manila leadership team has been trying to master a single move. We have practiced it day after day, week after week, month after month for many years.

The one move we have committed
ourselves to mastering is this:
a simple, biblical, transferable
discipleship process.

We have refused to let ourselves get off track pursuing fads, trends, traditions, or the latest get-big-quick schemes. We are determined, we are ruthlessly focused, and we are long past the consideration of learning other moves. That is not to say we are closed-minded to new disciple-making strategies. We consistently scan the horizon, searching for anything, anywhere that we should learn and incorporate. We read the books, listen to the podcasts, and send representatives to conferences and seminars all over the world. There are lots of good ministry ideas floating around. But in the final analysis, it always comes down to one question: Can that idea help us with our one move?

The one move we have committed ourselves to mastering is this: a simple, biblical, transferable discipleship process.

UNDERLINE
OR UNDERMINE?

Even though the term *discipleship process* is fairly descriptive, the meaning is often blurred. People try to get a handle on what we do by putting Victory–Manila in one of several well-known categories. I often find myself defining our process by contrasting it with what we are not. While we try to be friendly, we are not a seeker-friendly church like Willow Creek Community Church in Illinois. We hope we have a purpose, but we are not a "purpose-driven" church like Saddleback Church in California. We are not a cell church like the huge Korean and Singaporean cell churches. We are not a spiritual gifts church, a mystical prophetic church, a worship-centered church, a revival center, or a deeper-teaching church. We are not a preacher-based or even a cell-based church. There is nothing inherently good or bad about any of these growth strategies, and they may work for other churches. You may even periodically see some of those elements in what we do, but none of those approaches represents the basis of what we are about.

Ralph W. Neighbour, a longtime pastor and former missionary, is known in many circles as the brains behind the cell church movement of the 1990s. A few years ago at the peak of the cell church movement in Asia, one of Neighbour's assistants came to Manila while doing research for a book project. Having read several of Neighbour's books, I was truly honored to be interviewed. However, the interviewer and I never could get past a fundamental disagreement. He kept insisting that Victory was a cell church, and I kept insisting with equal conviction that it was not.

"Of course you are a cell church," he said. "Everyone is in a cell group—even the pastors. And, most important, cells are not just part of your church; they are the core. Therefore, Victory is a cell church, not a church with a cell program."

I tried in vain to explain that we are committed to an end product, while he seemed to be committed to a particular system or form. In other words, while we are all about making disciples, his chief concern was making cells, or small groups. It did not matter to him if the small groups were designed as holding tanks to keep fish from swimming back to sea or if they were designed to catch new fish. His primary concern was the structure. On the other hand, we use a cell structure only because it has proven to be an effective way to make disciples. If we ever find a better way to make disciples, we will abandon the small group structure immediately. This is because we are a discipleship-based church, not a cell-based church.

What I tried to explain was that our goal is to engage nonbelievers and help them become disciples of Jesus Christ. It is not about getting *church people into cells*; it is about *getting non-church people to Christ*. For us, small groups are only a means to an end for engaging our communities, establishing spiritual foundations, equipping believers to minister, and empowering disciples to make disciples.

The interviewer and I were still not connecting. As he walked out of my office, he called back, "No matter what you say, you are a cell church."

"No, we're a disciple-making church," I yelled. But he was already out the door.

It may seem to you that we were splitting hairs over minor points, but through the years Victory–Manila has become very clear and very focused on what we are trying to do. Why have we become so fixated on a single strategy? It is, first of all, because we have embraced the Lord's Great Commission as our own. Making disciples is the driving force behind everything we do. Second, it is because we have overwhelming confirmation in our own experience that this one move, if mastered, is unstoppable and indefensible—even if you are missing your left arm. I believe all churches and ministries can grow if only they master a discipleship process that is simple, biblical, and transferable. I know of churches that are missing many seemingly important things such as nice buildings, good music equipment, support staff, big givers, and dynamic preachers. Yet they are still growing because they are making disciples.

Churches can be blessed with all those seemingly important things and become completely consumed with activities that have nothing to do with making disciples. Our goal is to make our small groups and everything else we do support our discipleship process. Unfortunately, crowded church calendars often compete with discipleship. No activity is neutral. We recognize that everything we do and say will either *underline* or *undermine* our discipleship process.

STRATEGY 1.0— BIG-BANG EVENT EVANGELISM

To launch our original University Belt church in 1984, we conducted nightly evangelistic meetings for thirty straight nights. Because that was the way we did it in our US campus ministries, it was the only strategy I had ever known. Our main features were Rice Broocks's preaching, a multimedia rock 'n' roll exposé, and a minimally talented unknown Christian band. The advantage to us was that all three represented things no one else was doing in 1984 in the U-Belt. Rice Broocks is a dynamic evangelist who powerfully presents the gospel with his own unique brand of wit and humor. Between the band, the American team, and Rice, it was not difficult to draw a crowd and pack out our initial meeting place, the six-hundred-seat Girl Scouts Auditorium.

That actually became a problem because Christian youth groups in Manila began filling up vans and jeepneys (colorful vehicles used for public transportation) to haul their kids to our meetings. Each night Rice would ask who among the crowd were Christians and had come as a member of a church group. As graciously but as forcefully as he could, Rice would say, "We're glad you came, and we hope you learn something you can take with you. Go back to your church and be a blessing, but please do not come to these meetings. We simply do not have enough seats. We are here to reach lost Filipino students." We needed the Christians to stay away to make room for the student radicals and rioters.

When Rice and the American team moved on to South Korea, and Deborah and I were left behind, we obviously needed a new strategy. Years before arriving in the Philippines, I had learned not to try to imitate Rice's gifts and anointing. I knew I was not an evangelist, and I did not have the speaking skills to attract and keep a crowd. So we divided everyone into small groups and gave ourselves fully to establishing biblical foundations and equipping the young believers in basic ministry skills. It was a lot like a spiritual boot camp. The emphasis was on training young people to follow up and disciple the next wave of new believers. I was twenty-five years old and the oldest person in the group. For the first year, Deborah and I were the only married couple in our church.

We quickly fell into cycles of evangelism and follow-up. Rice or some other evangelist would visit Manila every three or four months for a series of meetings where Filipino students would receive Christ. That would be followed by several months of intensive foundational ministry. With every cycle, the "more mature" Filipino Christians—those who had been saved longer than a month—gained confidence and ministry experience. After all, they were spiritual giants compared to the "newbies."

For the next six years we continued with this growth strategy of event evangelism followed by intensive follow-up and discipleship. With that model we grew from 165 new believers to about 2,000.

MEASURING WHAT REALLY MATTERS

Every time I'm asked to teach a discipleship seminar, at some point I have to talk about the numbers. I always do so with some reluctance, but not because it is wrong to count members. My reluctance is due to people's common habit of attributing all kinds of virtue, worth, and wisdom to individuals and organizations based on how many people show up at their meetings. By those same calculations, there is a tendency to diminish the efforts of other leaders or churches because of their smallness. That is not fair because building a church of one hundred in Tokyo, Japan; Dhaka, Bangladesh; or the Iranian capital of Tehran takes more work and is a greater accomplishment than building a church of one thousand in Dallas, Singapore, or Manila. Some cities are ripe for harvest; others require serious plowing.

I came from a ministry that planted churches all over the world, but most were small. We may have had a couple of "megachurches" that grew to two hundred, but most had less than one hundred members. We were taught that we were small because we were really committed, and others were large because they had compromised on the terms of discipleship.

I suspect, however, that our frequent appeal to "quality, not quantity" was the *result* of our smallness, not the cause of it. In other words, we prided ourselves in quality simply because there was no quantity about which to boast. Even back then I could not help but wonder, "Why can't we have both quality and quantity?" In the many years since, I have seen small churches that had just as much compromise and immorality as big churches. I have also seen big churches with real disciples passionately following Jesus and fishing for men. What I have not seen is the automatic connection between smallness and depth or bigness and compromise.

Several points come to mind when I think about the ministry and numbers.

Every church, campus ministry, and discipleship group can grow.

When I was in high school, my family lived in Jackson, Mississippi, and we had a lake house outside of town. Every year we planted a huge garden. Tomatoes, jalapeños, green peppers, cucumbers, blueberries, blackberries—we planted everything that would grow in the hot, humid Mississippi summer. All that work would have made no sense unless we expected our work to bear fruit. Each year our garden produced enough vegetables to feed our whole neighborhood.

Doing ministry and doing church is much like planting that garden. The hard work is supposed to produce fruit. The apostle Paul wrote to the Corinthian church:

> I planted the seed, Apollos watered it, but God made it grow. So neither he who plants nor he who waters is anything, but only God, who makes

35

things grow. The man who plants and the man who waters have one purpose, and each will be rewarded according to his own labor.

—1 Corinthians 3:6–8

The three recurring words in this short passage are *plant*, *water*, and *grow*. The single purpose of planting and watering the seed (which is the Word of God) is that it will grow. If you do not expect the seed to grow, why plant it? As leaders, we must believe that our ministries will grow. It is hard to build a large disciple-making ministry if our mentality is scripted in smallness. Even in my early twenties, somehow I had it in my mind that I was supposed to reach thousands of people. I do not know exactly how that idea became so deeply implanted in me. There was nothing in my experience that provided that model. I came from a very small ministry in a very small town. I had never visited a large church, never met anyone who attended a large church, and didn't know anyone who led a large church. Nonetheless, somehow I knew that in order to reach this city of millions, small just would not do. I don't know where it came from, but this thought lodged itself in my brain: *As long as there is one unsaved person on my campus or in my city, then my church is not big enough.*

As long as there is one unsaved person on my campus or in my city, then my church is not big enough.

There are, of course, many Christian preachers and teachers who will boldly proclaim that growth is simply a matter of faith. They say, "If you believe it and if you can see it, then you can have it." That is the truth, but not necessarily the whole truth. In my years as a pastor I have encountered many leaders who dreamed big, confessed big, and talked big. They even tried to project bigness in their lifestyle with the idea that living large was an act of faith that would create a large and influential ministry. However, the reality was that though they were thinking big and living large, the way they were building almost guaranteed perpetual smallness.

Growth is not always easy to control. Every church or ministry is either organized for growth or organized for control.

At Victory–Manila we gave up on control a long time ago. It has been many years since I could approve or even know about every decision. These days I do not even know the names of many people on our staff, let alone the thousands of discipleship group leaders. To avoid losing control, some pastors decide to stay small. The reverse is more often the reality. When pastors determine to control everything, their ministries remain small as a consequence.

We cannot force or require people to make disciples, nor would we even try to do so. Likewise, we cannot control the speed and extent of our growth. We do not control people. However, we work hard to maintain and control the training system and process of making disciples. Where our church members and our disciple-making process take us is up to the Holy Spirit. At Victory, we had to come to the realization that if we pursue what God wants for the Philippines, we have to learn to live out of control.

There was a small but committed Christian fellowship back in Starkville where I went to college. That group, like the campus ministry I attended, was committed to making disciples, but unlike us, they seemed intentionally committed to smallness. They would talk about winning the town or the campus to Christ but never felt that they were spiritually ready. Their confession of faith was that one day they would come into a level of maturity, and then they would be ready to go and make disciples of the nations. Until then, they were simply making disciples of one another. When I visited Starkville fifteen years later, I discovered they were smaller than ever, still waiting to get mature enough to engage the community and grow.

The growth rate has a lot to do with the soil.

I have many fond childhood memories of picking blueberries with my parents and siblings at our family lake house. We had countless blueberry bushes that required no maintenance and produced more blueberries than we could possibly pick or eat each summer. So when my wife and I bought a home in Nashville a few years ago, one of the first things I did was plant blueberries in our backyard.

The guy who sold me the bushes warned me that the soil in Nashville was not acidic enough for blueberries to thrive, but that I could improve the situation by adding ammonium sulfate to the soil. I did everything I was told to do, but within a year all my blueberry bushes were dead. There was nothing wrong with the water, the blueberry bushes, or the sunlight.

The soil was the problem. It is the same with ministry and the seed of God's Word.

Victory–Manila has grown to tens of thousands, while our church in Bangladesh has only reached in the hundreds. Those hundreds, however, represent a huge church in light of Bangladesh being a traditionally Muslim nation. Jesus always looked beyond the numbers themselves. The master in Jesus's parable of the talents rejoiced just as much over the two talents growing to four as he did the ten talents growing to twenty. Jesus also said the angels rejoice more over one coming to repentance than ninety-nine who need no repentance. (See Matthew 18:12–13.) Jesus rejoiced more over the two coins the poor woman gave than the large gifts from the wealthy. (See Mark 12:43–44.)

You cannot judge the quality of a church or a person's ministry simply by how many attend the weekend worship service. I have determined not to be impressed by numbers, especially our own. Weekend attendance can be one of the most unreliable indicators of the health of a church because looking at the raw numbers does not account for the condition of the soil.

REVERSE TRENDING

Something ought to be said here about the Filipino soil in which we are planting and watering God's Word. It would be easy to simply attribute Victory's growth in the last twenty-seven years to Filipino church growth trends in general. Actually, since my wife and I began leading Victory–Manila we have not followed the trends but have consistently moved in the opposite direction.

Along with twenty thousand other churches, Victory is part of the Philippine Council of Evangelical Churches (PCEC). I have been a columnist for their magazine since the nineties. Being connected with that organization, our team has had access to some brilliant church leaders who keep statistics on everything related to church health and growth. There have been some interesting trends through the years. The turmoil of the eighties seemed to have been a catalyst for growth in most Filipino churches. In that decade almost anything that represented an idea about God grew quickly. By comparison, Victory–Manila's growth from 1984 through 1990 was anything but phenomenal. We actually grew at a rate much slower than many other churches.

By the 1990s, the economy was recovering, and church growth in the Philippines was beginning to slow and flatten. By the late 1990s, some larger churches were in gradual decline. In contrast, Victory grew slowly when everyone else seemed to be exploding. When Filipino church growth was flat in the 1990s, Victory–Manila began to explode. Then in the 2000s, when church attendance was in decline in many megachurches, Victory's growth rate spun out of control. From 1984 to 1990, Victory grew from 165 to about 2,000. From 1990 to 2000, Victory grew from 2,000 to 4,900. By 2011, we had grown from 4,900 to more than 52,000 attending one of eighty-one worship services meeting in one of fifteen metro Manila locations.

There are several important points that can be made about those numbers, perhaps the most important being this: Though growing from 165 to 52,000 may sound impressive, had we not made some significant philosophical and structural changes from around 1991 to 1993, we would have probably followed the trend of many other churches in the Philippines—flat growth and financial difficulties. In our first six years (1984 to 1990), we were tracking behind the trend as it was. In the following two decades, perhaps we could have maintained the 2,000 and maybe even bucked the trend and grown a little. But there is no way we would have seen the exponential growth since 1991 without shifting from a model dependent on big-bang event evangelism to a small group discipleship model.

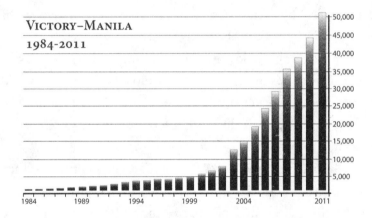

SOMETIMES THE NUMBERS LIE

There were two factors that forced us to make philosophical changes in the Victory strategy. The first was physical. In 1988, at the four-year mark, we had two congregations in Manila, and I was leading both of them. I had never heard of multi-site churches. When people heard I was leading "one church in two locations," they looked at me as if I were crazy or confused. Maybe I was a little of both. Today there are scores of books, blogs, and podcasts on multisite ministry designed to help pastors avoid all the mistakes we made. I sure wish that stuff had been available in 1988. Maybe I would have fewer wrinkles and more hair.

At that time we were experiencing what I thought of as explosive growth. Twelve hundred people were attending, and we had planted a few other churches in the Philippine provinces and overseas. It was at that point I had a strange health breakdown. Somehow I picked up an amoeba that should have incapacitated me for only a week or two. After one month, however, I was still sick. Two then three months went by, and I was no better. From Sunday afternoon each week through the following Saturday night, I was often too sick to leave the house. The next Sunday somehow I would revive, get up, preach three times in our two locations, and collapse for the rest of the week. None of the doctors I visited could figure out what was wrong with me.

In almost everyone's eyes I was a successful pastor. They could see the proof of it in our numbers. But that was where the numbers lied, at least the numbers most people were viewing. We were making a lot of disciples, but the process was killing me. The way things were going I would not have been able to continue much longer. Contrary to how some people interpreted the numbers, we were not a healthy church. In the midst of all the good that was happening, the way we were doing things was cultivating the seeds of our own destruction.

"HI, MY NAME IS STEVE, AND I'M A WORKAHOLIC"

Finally I met with a doctor who asked, "Steve, what do you do for a living? What does your weekly schedule look like?" After a few moments of questions and answers where I laid out the nature and scope of my work, he was convinced.

"Wow! Have you ever heard of stress?" he asked. "The human body is not designed to work at your pace. You need to change your lifestyle. You need to take care of your body. Exercise, rest, eat right, take a vacation."

Vacation. Rest. Exercise. Those were concepts I had rejected in my mad rush to save the world, one disciple at a time.

About this time our good friends Pastor John and Maretta Rohrer invited Deborah and me to Melbourne, Australia, to teach in their church missions conference. I preached twice, and then our friends kidnapped us for two weeks of chasing kangaroos, lying on the beach, and watching old black-and-white movies. I returned to Manila completely "healed" and restored and with the energy to get back to work—but this time with a little balance.

There was a second factor that forced us to begin thinking about a major shift in the way we were doing church. What seemed to be a great church-planting opportunity turned into a struggle that revealed some serious cracks in our ministry strategy. I received a call from a friend of a friend who had recently given his life to Christ. He was the owner of the Star Complex theater in the Shangri-La Mall. The former movie theater had been converted into a one-thousand-seat facility designed for stage plays, musicals, and concerts. Now this new believer wanted to give the theater to God (although he charged us rent) so someone could start a church there. The man was told, "Call Steve Murrell. He'll start a church anywhere."

Because we were out of space in our Makati Sports Club location, using the theater sounded like a good idea and an answer to prayer. So I asked one hundred Makati people to help us plant a new congregation by sleeping late on Sunday and bringing their friends to a 4:00 p.m. service at the Star Complex. One hundred worshipers in a one-thousand-seat theater is not exactly a compelling environment for growth, but within one year we were packed with standing-room-only attendance. This was another instance of numbers telling lies. The more we grew, the more problems manifested themselves.

Our congregation at the Star Complex was very different from our other congregations. Our first congregation in Manila's U-Belt on Recto Avenue was founded with new believers from the student riots in 1984. At that time we were so determined to win new people to Christ, not to recruit other Christians, that Rice had run off all the youth groups looking for an inspiring Christian meeting. The Makati congregation was likewise birthed through evangelism. However, our Star Complex adventure at the Shangri-La Mall was different. Maybe the name was prophetic. The idea of a "Shangri-La" paradise runs a bit counter to discipleship, and "Star Complex" certainly does not imply cross-carrying self-sacrifice. It took us awhile to realize what was going on. We had birthed our Star Complex congregation by simply attracting Christians from other churches. It was not intentional. It's just what happens when you combine a convenient location with good music and slightly above-average preaching.

LEARNING FROM OUR MISTAKES

Though the tenfold growth in attendance might have suggested to many that great things were happening, something was fundamentally wrong. Whenever we took up an offering, there would be notes in the baskets complaining about my preaching, my informal dress, the length of our youth pastor's hair, and so on. Any and every aspect of the ministry received critiques, complaints, a few demands, and usually some references to how things were done in a former church. That year of impressive growth turned out to be the most miserable year of my entire ministry.

I knew something was wrong,
but I had no clue how to fix it.

One Sunday afternoon, while driving home from Shangri-La after preaching to a crowded theater with every seat filled, people sitting on the floor, and others standing shoulder to shoulder along the walls, I heard the same words that Jethro spoke to Moses, only I think God was speaking them to me: "What you are doing is not good" (Exod. 18:17). I had no argument. I knew something was wrong, but I had no clue how to fix it.

Good definitely came out of the mistakes and frustrations

of that year. Some precious people joined the church that year, but something was amiss. The Victory leadership team and I were forced to step back and take a long, hard look at what we were doing—at our discipleship process and our strategy for reaching the lost. We had not intentionally tried to recruit religious church people to the Shangri-La congregation any more than we had in the early days at the U-Belt. There was, however, a difference. In our early days at the U-Belt we were completely focused on winning the lost and quickly making disciples to replace ourselves. Everyone on the American team knew his or her time was short. That single-minded commitment made Rice's plea for the youth groups to stay away seem like the perfectly natural thing to do.

Most church planters do not set out to recruit other Christians as the foundation of their church. In many cultures there is no need; it happens automatically if you just let it. The fact that we let it happen at Shangri-La was evidence that we had no clear strategy for winning lost people to Christ. The Shangri-La debacle taught us that excellent worship, decent preaching, and a cool venue would attract Christians looking for a more meaningful church experience. It also taught us that non-Christians really do not care about those things, and they proved it by staying away.

Prior to and during the whole Shangri-La experience, my good friend Luther Mancao constantly pestered our leadership team with his cell church books and tapes (the 1990s version of podcasts). After seeing our mistakes, we were finally ready to listen and try out Luther's ideas. As we began to gradually shift our emphasis from big events to small group discipleship, we all felt we were about to stumble into something big.

As Luther predicted, it took about two years to transition our church from a Sunday meeting culture to a small group discipleship culture that operated twenty-four hours a day, seven days a week.

During the long transition we had several false starts and learned many important lessons the hard way. For almost two years we said nothing from the pulpit about the change. All of our pastors and staff simply started making disciples in small groups. When someone would hear about a small group and ask if they could join, we would tell them, "No, you can't join one, but if you will gather three church friends and three unchurched friends, we will teach you how to lead one. When would you like to start?" We created what I called a "top-down, grassroots discipleship movement" within our church. At this point, our multisite church was meeting in three Manila venues—the U-Belt, Makati Sports Club, and Shangri-La's Star Complex.

As we began to make significant philosophical changes in the way we would do church, there was no small amount of research, prayer, and discussion among the Victory leadership team. When the concern arose about how to organize the church into small discipleship groups, we finally realized that the organizing did not matter. We knew that it would be impossible to get everyone to buy into the new structure. Some would get it immediately; others eventually; some never. We decided we would build a small group discipleship system for the ten thousand we had not yet reached, not for the two thousand we had already reached. That single-minded passion for the lost has always been the motive behind every part of Victory's discipleship vision.

COUNTING WHAT REALLY COUNTS

There is nothing wrong with numbers and nothing wrong with using them to carefully measure progress. The important thing is figuring out which numbers are the key indicators— those numbers that are most important because they are the best measure of what you are called to do. The philosophical change at Victory–Manila gave birth to a new system for making disciples that changed what we counted. Michael E. Gerber, management guru and author of the popular *E-Myth* books said, "For ordinary people to do extraordinary things, a system—'a way of doing things'—is absolutely essential."[1]

I see the evidence of this every day I am in the Philippines. One of the underlying principles of our discipleship strategy is that every believer can and should make disciples. And we've built a system—a way of doing things—to make it happen. As a leadership team we focus most of our attention on building, monitoring, and maintaining a simple process that equips and empowers even the youngest of Christians to make new disciples. That is why for many years I have been able to leave the country for months at a time, and when I return the church is always larger.

"For ordinary people to do extraordinary things, a system—'a way of doing things'—is absolutely essential." —Michael E. Gerber

It is important to identify the key indicators that truly measure progress and success. It does not help if we are counting the wrong numbers or attributing some kind of meaning to numbers that don't really matter. After we determine which statistics are significant, then what we measure becomes a true reflection of the church's progress.

When we shifted from an event evangelism approach to a small group discipleship focus at Victory, it was reflected in a new way of counting. In other words, we had a different way of measuring and defining success. We were no longer satisfied just to have a crowd on Sunday and a good offering. We learned to count the things that really matter. So here they are, the four things we are primarily concerned about at Victory–Manila and therefore count:

1. Victory discipleship groups

While it is possible to lead a small group and not actually make disciples, and it is possible to make disciples without a small group, I am convinced that the most efficient and effective way to make disciples is in small groups. After all, that is how Jesus did it, and who am I to think that I can improve on His system? Because we value discipleship, we count the number of active small groups.

2. Victory Weekend

This is a retreat where we concentrate on establishing biblical foundations such as faith, repentance, baptism, and an understanding of the cross. Because foundations matter, we count the number of Victory Weekends and the number of participants.

3. Making Disciples and Training for Victory

Because the primary job of full-time ministry staff is not to do ministry but to equip God's people to do ministry, an intentional equipping track is essential. "Making Disciples" is a four-hour class that presents the basics of how Victory small groups operate. Similarly, "Training for Victory" is a ten-week intensive equipping course that prepares anyone to make disciples by starting, leading, or simply participating in a church-based small group.

4. Weekend worship attendance

Like all churches, we methodically count how many people show up at our worship services. However, this number is the least important of all the numbers we track. There are several reasons why this number is not our chief concern. First of all, each worship service lasts only seventy to ninety minutes and is a time primarily for worship and a sermon. Obviously, if we were depending on that moment to plant, water, and cultivate the seed of God's Word in people's lives, we would hardly have time to get the plow in the ground.

Our goal is not to grow in attendance but to make disciples. Too many churches are more concerned with membership and attendance than with discipleship. Being at church on Sunday is important, but being the church Monday through Saturday is more important. Real discipleship happens twenty-four hours a day, seven days a week, not just on Sundays.

WIKICHURCH LESSONS

I wish I could say it was a strategic discovery based on much prayer and research, but the fact is, I actually stumbled onto the foundational principle that revolutionized my life and ministry. Here it is: no matter what is missing from your church or campus ministry, if you master just one move—making disciples in small groups—you will be unstoppable. It's as simple as planting the seed of God's Word. How quickly that seed grows depends, to a large degree, on the soil in which the seed is planted.

Do not let the numbers intimidate, impress, or confuse you. If you are ministering in a hard place such as Japan or Pakistan, if you have a small congregation, or if you are launching a new church plant, a much smaller number can represent an equally miraculous harvest. A WikiChurch's job is to make disciples. God causes the growth, but we must be careful to aim at and hit the right target.

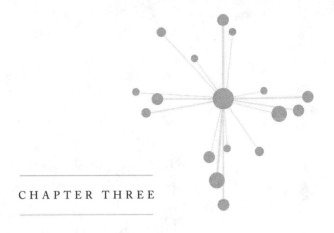

CHAPTER THREE

HITTING THE
WRONG TARGET

W ITH A GOLD medal already in the bag, American shooter Matt Emmons was one shot away from double gold in the 2004 Athens Olympics. Matt was at the top of his game. He had already won the International Shooting Sport Federation Championship in 2002 and 2004. His final target was fifty meters away. Sitting in first place, all he had to do was hit the target for his second gold. Matt sighted the target, took a deep breath, and squeezed the trigger.

Bang! Dead center. And with that shot Matt went from a gold medal to eighth place. That's what happens when you make a perfect shot—at the wrong target.[1]

I don't know any pastors or missionaries who do not want to make disciples. But many well-meaning people are taking their best shots but aiming at the wrong targets simply because they have wrongly defined discipleship. They are busy doing traditional church activities, running the latest slick programs, and generally doing everything that can be done in the name of God except making disciples. It seems many leaders are shooting at and hitting every target that moves, but few of the targets have anything to do with discipleship. Being focused on everything is the same as being focused on nothing.

DEFINING
THE TARGET

Several years ago a pastor of relatively large American church asked me speak to his small group leaders. He had visited Victory–Manila and was impressed with the seemingly inexhaustible supply of small group leaders. What really got his attention was that our volunteers seemed to actually enjoy making disciples and doing ministry. I told my friend, "I am not sure I'm the speaker you want talking to your leaders. You seem to have a good thing going, and I don't want to mess it up."

I explained that my chief concern was that speaking to his leaders on the details of what we do at Victory–Manila could inject confusion into his leadership team. To put it another way, our respective leadership teams were not aiming at the same target. Nonetheless, my friend persisted. "What we are doing is not working," he said. "Our cell leaders are burning out and quitting all the time. Something has to change, but I'm not sure what. Please help us."

After several cautions and with my warning clearly issued, I agreed to spend a day with his small group leaders.

"So, explain to me," I said to the pastor, "what it is you are trying to do and how you are trying to do it."

My friend had a considerable number of visitors coming to the church, and many of them were making decisions for Christ. However, an equal number were disappearing, and consequently the church was not growing. His objective was to use small groups to "close the back door." He went on to explain various aspects of his system. The congregation was divided into geographic regions. On Wednesday evenings, small groups consisting of church members at all age levels met in each of those zip code regions. The leaders were all mature Christian couples. The meetings consisted of praise, worship, and a message developed by the small group leaders.

When it was my turn to explain the process at Victory, I simply said, "Take everything you do, and imagine the exact opposite. That is basically how we do it. For us there is no set time or place for discipleship groups. They meet any day of the week, any place, and at any time. A few meet in homes; most of our successful ones do not. Some begin as early as 6:00 a.m., and some meet after midnight. Couples are rarely the leaders because in our culture, men disciple men and women disciple women. We have small group leaders in their eighties and leaders who are teenagers. We do not sing or take up offerings in our small groups. Leaders work from materials the pastoral team has created, usually based on the weekend sermon. Our Victory small groups are the front door to the church, not the back door."

How can two highly motivated, well-intended Christian leaders set out to make disciples and come up with the exact opposite approaches? In this case, it had nothing to do with creating different systems in order to effectively engage our very different cultures. These two processes that headed in two different directions were simply the inevitable result of two different ideas about the definition and target of the discipleship process. For my friend and his leadership team, the discipleship process was designed to take care of the faithful, and their goal for small groups was to close the back door. For us, small groups are the front door to the church, and discipleship begins with nonbelievers.

---

*A successful disciple–making process
is not developed overnight.*

Different ideas about discipleship are common. Ask twenty different people across the body of Christ to define discipleship, and you might get forty different answers. A church's process of making disciples is inevitably an outgrowth of their leadership's definition of discipleship. In other words, how you try to make disciples is determined by what you think a disciple is. Turn it around and look at it from the other end. The process we develop for making disciples is a reflection of what we really believe about discipleship. It shows not only what we think Christian discipleship should look like, but it also reveals how clearly or how seriously we embrace Jesus's Great Commission to go into all the world and make disciples.

I seem to have been placed in a unique position from which to communicate and assist hundreds of other Christian leaders trying to crack the mission codes for their own communities and cultures. Like that of our church, their goal is to find a process that will effectively engage nonbelievers in their community. And like our church, they are trying to create a discipleship culture and process that will multiply rather than add.

I have seen leaders who have been quite successful and others who have floundered unsuccessfully trying one system after another. A successful disciple-making process is not developed overnight. Ours has been evolving for decades. Some things have worked for us, and others have not. When a discipleship process fails, many times the fatal flaw is that the definition of discipleship is either unclear, unbiblical, or not commonly shared by the leadership team. A clearly defined and commonly shared definition of discipleship is important because it is a starting point for creating an integrated, effective process of making disciples.

DEFINING THE D-WORD

What is discipleship, anyway? Of all that can be said about discipleship, it is first and foremost simple. It may not sound spiritual, but simplicity is vitally important. *The more exclusive and complex discipleship becomes, the further it is removed from what Jesus did and from what He commanded us to do.*

Complexity is one of the main hindrances for many churches wanting to create a multiplying discipleship process.

If a person who makes disciples is thought of as a super-Christian or a spiritual sage, and if the goal of discipleship is to make other super-Christians or spiritual sages, then few will even attempt to make disciples. In that case, a quickly multiplying process is out of the question.

Of course, Jesus could be considered the Sage of sages. However, He selected the simplest, most ordinary people for His first discipleship group. Obviously what He wanted to teach them could not have been all that complicated. Difficult? Yes. Complicated? Absolutely not!

So exactly what is discipleship?

Discipleship is a call to follow Jesus.

The starting point of being a disciple is the decision to follow Jesus. A rich and powerful young businessman who had obtained all that the world could offer came to Jesus wanting to know how he could also gain eternal life. After some discussion about keeping the Law, the young man was still unsatisfied. "All these I have kept since I was a boy," he said. Jesus finally said to him, "You still lack one thing. Sell everything you have and give to the poor, and you will have treasure in heaven. Then come, follow me" (Luke 18:21–22). The rich guy was saddened by Jesus's response. He was a man of great wealth, and the cost of following Jesus was just too high.

"Following Jesus" is one of those religious phrases that is used so much that we forget what it means. Common phrases, especially common religious phrases, tend to lose their true meaning and impact over time. Just ask the CEO Christians (those who attend church on "Christmas and Easter only") if they are followers of Jesus. Many might sincerely say they are. There is a considerable gap between what following Jesus means to them and what it meant to the rich young ruler. It is possible to believe in Jesus and still not follow Him. It is even possible to be a good church member and yet not really follow Jesus.

The idea of following Jesus can also be a little bewildering to nonbelievers. After all, how do you follow a person around if you cannot even see him? Following Jesus means that we believe His words, imitate His character, and obey His commands. Following Jesus is, however, more than simply being a good person. As illustrated in the passage above, to follow Jesus means to surrender our lives and our wills to follow His. Jesus put it this way: "If anyone would come after me, he must deny himself and take up his cross and follow me" (Matt. 16:24).

Anyone can disciple others as long as he or she is sincerely endeavoring to follow Christ.

Although Jesus and the twelve disciples provide our model of Christian discipleship, there is one key difference. The twelve were followers of the discipleship group leader, who was Jesus Himself. In our model of discipleship at Victory, people are not considered the disciples and followers of a group leader, but disciples and followers of Jesus. That is not just a matter of how we express it but how we think of it.

Discipleship is learning from other disciples as we follow Christ together. That greatly simplifies the role of a discipleship group leader. Anyone can disciple others as long as he or she is sincerely endeavoring to follow Christ.

Discipleship is a call to "fish" for people.

Jesus explained the specific goal for His followers when He said, "Follow Me, and I will make you fishers of people." (See Matthew 4:19.) Back in our college days Rice used to talk about the "Christian ghetto," meaning the places where Christian students hung out to isolate themselves from the real world that included "sinners" on campus. Following Jesus does not mean we cut off all contact with our nonreligious friends. Rather we should continue in our relationships so that Christ's love can flow through us to others. Matthew the tax collector is a great example of this. As soon as Matthew answered the call to follow Jesus, he threw a party at his house so all his old friends could meet Jesus and his new friends.

The religious leaders were upset that Jesus and His disciples went to Matthew's party, and "they asked his disciples, 'Why does your teacher eat with tax collectors and "sinners"?'" (Matt. 9:11). Assume for a moment that not all Pharisees were hypocrites. Some were sincere in their devotion to God, and many did eventually become followers of Christ. Pharisees defined right standing with God not only in terms of the works of the Law but also in terms of separation. And they made their own disciples by teaching them a very long list of rules on how to be separate. As I said previously, your definition of discipleship creates your disciple-making process. You can see why even the sincere Pharisees had such a hard time with Jesus. Engaging nonbelievers and sinners went against all of their customs and beliefs.

Imagine a doctor who gets offended with sick people. "I am committed to health," the doctor says. "How dare you bring your sickness into my office."

"But I don't feel well. Can you help me?"

"No, I am dedicated to helping people stay healthy."

"But well people don't need any help."

"Right. That's why we quarantine sick people like you—so you won't infect us."

Look at how Jesus responded to the Pharisees' question "Why does your teacher eat with tax collectors and sinners?"

> It is not the healthy who need a doctor, but the sick. But go and learn what this means: "I desire mercy, not sacrifice." For I have not come to call the righteous, but sinners.
>
> —MATTHEW 9:12

Jesus was not going to let these Pharisees off the hook regarding their attitude toward people they considered sinners. Their separation could not be excused on the basis of simply not knowing how to relate or because they had inherited a faulty definition of discipleship. They were not engaging sinners, Jesus charged, because they lacked compassion. In other encounters with the Pharisees, Jesus added pride and self-righteousness to the indictment.

I once heard a podcast interview with Rick Warren, pastor of one of the largest churches in America. Rick was asked how he encourages his congregation to participate in personal evangelism, considering how many people come to Christ at

Saddleback Church. Rick's response was interesting. He said Saddleback has never instituted a formal evangelism program. Instead he tells people, "Write down what you love to do most, and then go do it with unbelievers....Whatever you love to do, turn it into an outreach."

Rick went on to explain that they tell new believers that if they love to play bridge, they should keep playing bridge—just with unbelievers. If they enjoy watching Monday night football, they should keep watching Monday night football, as long as they invite over their nonchurch friends. He said that if we stay engaged in our relationships, then it is only a matter of time until we have an opportunity to share the story of our faith journey. Maybe a friend will mention his economic woes or his frustration with his teenager. Both are open doors to offer prayer, our testimony, or some humble godly wisdom. Just keep the relationships, pray for your friends, and wait for open doors.[2]

Separated Christians quickly forget how to relate to non-believers. It happens almost automatically without a consistent effort to befriend and build relationships outside the church. A good example of how "professional Christians" lose the ability to relate was displayed on a sign I saw in front of a huge Nashville church. It read, "Sinners Welcome!" I thought to myself as I drove by, "Yeah, that'll really bring 'em in. There must be thousands of unchurched people out there who cannot wait to visit a group of self-righteous, religious people willing to allow a few sinners to visit their church."

One thing is clear from the story of Jesus calling a tax collector to follow Him: Jesus's strategy of making disciples was not calling the already religious to follow Him. Instead of separating Himself from nonbelievers, Jesus came to be known as a friend of sinners, and He called them to be His followers.

If you have been a Christian for a while, and if you have been exposed to various definitions of discipleship across the body of Christ, you probably noticed something different in the first two chapters of this book. When I talk about discipleship, making disciples, discipleship culture, or a discipleship-based ministry strategy, it always begins with nonbelievers. Discipleship, in our understanding, is not a mentoring program to help encourage Christians to become better Christians. The discipleship process starts with introducing nonbelievers to the gospel and person of Jesus Christ.

It is quite amazing how consistently Christians, particularly Western Christians, divorce evangelism from discipleship. There are scores of discipleship programs designed to train and mature believers. In some there is an appendix in the back with an explanation of the gospel. This is included in the event that a nonbeliever accidentally slips into a discipleship group.

When Jesus told His disciples to go and make disciples of all the nations, none of them thought He meant for them to gather up all those who already believed and start little discipleship groups. That is certainly not what He intended and certainly not what they did. We are under no illusion that we can make disciples of the nations—or the Philippines or Manila or our neighborhoods or our friends—without consistently engaging nonbelievers.

You might say that what we do in our small groups is evangelism, but we think of it as simply the first step in the discipleship process. It really does not matter what you call it; the only thing that matters is what you do. The right definition of discipleship is the foundation of any discipleship strategy. When we separate the Siamese twins of evangelism and discipleship, we kill both. The biblical starting point of discipleship is evangelism, and the whole point of evangelism is to make disciples.

Discipleship is a call to fellowship with others.

When Jesus called Matthew to follow Him, Matthew had to follow along with Peter and John. He was not given the option of following Jesus alone. Contrary to Western evangelicalism's obsession with the individual, discipleship is and always has been a group project. No one in the New Testament followed independent of other followers. Their faith was lived in community with other followers. This community of believers has been described with many words such as *brotherhood*, *spiritual family*, and *covenant community*. The most common in the Bible is *fellowship*. In its simplest definition, fellowship is a Christ-centered relationship.

Biblical fellowship is more than greeting a few church members in the lobby, and it is certainly more than being someone's online contact. Real fellowship can only happen in a community of believers. Jesus would occasionally take one of His disciples aside for a private conversation, but one-on-one discipleship was not His main strategy. He discipled the twelve as a group. There is no greater setting in which people grow in faith, character, and wisdom than a small group.

WHAT DISCIPLESHIP IS NOT

Having written a brief definition of what discipleship is to Victory, I need to address a few misunderstandings by pointing out what discipleship is not. First of all, discipleship has nothing to do with spiritual authority. Every time I hear authority mentioned in the context of discipleship, I get worried. Eventually, bad things are going to happen if they have not already. In Matthew 28:19, Jesus commissioned His disciples to "go and make disciples of all nations." However, He prefaced the Great Commission with these words: "All authority in heaven and on earth has been given to me" (v. 18).

Here is my paraphrase of that verse: "You guys are going out to make disciples," Jesus says. "The people you disciple will in turn make other disciples. Now, let's get something straight from the beginning. You are to make disciples and teach people everything I taught you. But remember that all authority is Mine; it has been given to Me by My Father."

If all authority is His, then how much is ours? Let me put it another way. If all the money in my wallet is mine, how much is yours? Right. None. So, again, if all authority is His, how much is ours? Right again. None. Discipleship is not an authority trip. It is a process to help someone follow Jesus.

DANGER ZONE: PROCEED WITH CAUTION

I grew up in a rural state in the southern United States where guns were as common as baseball bats and hunting was a way of life. The rule was that we had to eat whatever we killed.

For boys who were inclined to shoot anything that moved, that rule gave one a reason to pause before firing away. My brothers and I were drilled thoroughly on the dangers and proper use of guns before we were even allowed to touch one. I cannot imagine handing a gun to a twelve-year-old without warnings, rules, and restrictions. Likewise, before you begin to disciple someone or send out others to make disciples, you need to get clear on the issue of spiritual authority because authority, like a gun, can be dangerous when not handled properly.

Do not think for a second that discipling involves one person having spiritual authority over another. In several Gospel passages Jesus gave His disciples authority to heal diseases and cast out demons (Matt. 10:1; Mark 6:7; Luke 9:1). But Jesus was equally clear that when His disciples made other disciples, they were not to be like pagan leaders who were authority-mongers. At one point Jesus called His disciples together and said to them, "You know that the rulers of the Gentiles lord it over them, and their high officials exercise authority over them" (Matt. 20:25). In contrast, Jesus told His disciples to become as the lowest, as the servant.

All of Jesus's teachings to His disciples in the first century apply to us in the twenty-first century. As Jesus's disciples, we still have authority over diseases and demonic forces, and we still proclaim with authority the words of Jesus and the witness of the apostles. At the same time, regarding spiritual authority over other people, the ultimate authority still belongs to Jesus alone.

You may be thinking to yourself, "What about scriptures that refer to authority given to bishops, pastors, and church elders?" (See 2 Corinthians 10:8; 13:10; Titus 2:15; Hebrews 13:17.) These instances refer to senior church leaders and to their organizational and instructional leadership. In no way should these verses relating to official church leadership be used to infuse spiritual authority into a discipleship relationship.

ACCOUNTABLE TO WHOM?

Second, discipleship is not about human accountability. When I was a new believer, the guy who led me to the Lord would ask me every week whether I had read my Bible each day since our last meeting. He did not stop with Bible reading. He asked about my relationship with my parents, my language, what I did on a Saturday night, and if I treated my girlfriend as Christ would treat her. He was a Presbyterian youth pastor and must have been a direct descendant of the early Puritans. As a brand-new believer who knew nothing about the Bible or what it meant to follow Christ, I needed that accountability.

A Filipino businessman in my discipleship group shared with me a prayer concern about an upcoming business trip. The destination was Bangkok, and wives were not invited. It did not take a prophet to see what could happen on that trip. I really did pray for my friend, but I also told him that upon his return I was going to look him right in the eye and ask him if he had remained faithful to Christ and to his wife.

We can and should have people in our lives at critical moments and in particular situations to hold us accountable in light of our weaknesses. Many people are trying to overcome some form of addictive behavior and for a season need a degree of human accountability. We have professional counselors in our church who work with people in those situations. However, the intent of the guy who first discipled me was to teach me how to be *accountable to God*. That was my intent with my friend who went to Bangkok as well. If discipleship helps me to be accountable to God, then that's a good thing. But so-called discipleship that makes people dependent on and accountable to another human completely misses the point. Discipleship is first and foremost about following Jesus.

All authority, all accountability, and all judgment have been given to Christ. It is to Him that every knee shall bow, and every tongue will acknowledge His authority as King of kings and Lord of lords. The goal of discipleship is to teach people to observe the things that Jesus commanded and submit life's decisions to Him, not to a small group leader who is discipling them.

In the end it does not matter whether I gave my youth pastor an account of my weekly Bible reading or whether my friend gave me a report about his trip to Bangkok. Hebrews 4:13 says, "Nothing in all creation is hidden from God's sight. Everything is uncovered and laid bare before the eyes of him to whom we must give account." Jesus said, "There is nothing concealed that will not be disclosed, or hidden that will not be made known. What I tell you in the dark, speak in the daylight; what is whispered in your ear, proclaim from the roofs" (Matt. 10:26–27). Paul wrote to the Romans, "Each of us will give an account of himself to God" (Rom. 14:12). The goal of discipleship is to teach God's Word and in doing so make people aware of their accountability—not to us, but to God.

DISCIPLESHIP
IS RELATIONSHIP

There are many different ways to describe discipleship and the discipleship process. How does this one sound to you? A biblically sound and theologically correct New Testament discipleship model strategically and intentionally attempts to create an organic, culturally relevant, self-replicating system of making disciples according to precise definitions and measurable goals.

If you think that sounds way too mechanical, you are absolutely right. The simplest but most profound way to define discipleship is to understand it in terms of relationship. Discipleship is about building three key relationships: first with God (follow), then with nonbelievers (fish), and finally with God's people (fellowship).

We did not begin our discipleship program with a complex system, a list of job descriptions, or an organizational chart, and neither should you. We began with sincere and authentic relationships. In other words, we actually cared about people. That is how we started, and it continues to be the foundation of all we do. The constantly evolving discipleship process we use has grown *out of* relationships and continues to grow *because* of relationships. That is not to suggest that relationships are easy; they are not. We are constantly thinking, praying, studying, and evaluating how we relate to God, to our community, and to our church family.

For each church leadership team that sets out to create a system for making disciples, the first thing that needs to be evaluated—or perhaps radically changed—is not existing systems but existing relationships. First, how is your relationship with God (follow)? Are you really following Jesus? Second, how are your relationships with nonbelievers (fish)? Are you really engaging your community and your culture? Have you as a disciple become a fisher for men? Third, how are your relationships in the body of Christ as a whole and in your own local church (fellowship)?

An effective disciple-making culture does not create or maintain itself. However, if those three key relationships that define a disciple of Jesus are working properly, then it is difficult to keep disciples from multiplying and churches from growing. In fact, if our systems are not working, if our church is not growing, if we are not making disciples, if the disciples are not maturing and bearing fruit by making other disciples, it always goes back to one of these relationship issues. The same thing applies to leadership, funding, serving, relating to other ministries, and every other aspect of a healthy, growing church. It all goes back to relationships with God, with people in the world, and with God's people.

What is true for starting a church or implementing a simple discipleship strategy is still true for us at Victory–Manila. We recognize that if we carefully maintain the well-oiled, finely tuned disciple-making process that has evolved in the Philippines but allow the relationships that created it to diminish, then we would become a shell of our original selves—the form without the power.

Remember Matt Emmons, the Olympian who hit the wrong target? After his humiliating last shot, he retreated to an Athens pub to forget about his failure. While in the pub he was approached by Kateřina Kurkova, a member of the Czech

Olympic shooting team, who introduced herself and tried to encourage him after his failure. One thing led to another, and they are now Matt and Katy Emmons.[3]

Matt may have missed the gold, but he got the girl. He hit the wrong target, but in the end he got something better than an Olympic medal. He got a relationship.

WikiChurch Lessons

So, what is discipleship anyway? Discipleship is relationship on three levels—with God, with nonbelievers, and with believers. Get those three things right, and you are a WikiChurch that will eventually go viral. Even if you miss a few targets and don't achieve all your number goals, it's OK because, ultimately, discipleship is measured in terms of relationships.

CHAPTER FOUR

THE POWER OF PROCESS

DISCIPLESHIP IS NOT an event, encounter, or an experience. It is an ongoing process. Great spiritual experiences alone do not necessarily produce disciples who are following Christ, fishing for men, and fellowshiping with other followers. Two experiences from my early days as a Christian illustrate the importance of a simple disciple-making process.

Although I lived in one of the most religious cities in America, I grew up in a not-so-religious family. When I was young, my dad was a deeply dedicated man, devoted more than anything else to his Sunday morning tee time. Rain or shine, freezing cold or one hundred degrees, if the golf course was open, he was there. We didn't go to church very often, but we never missed midnight Mass on Christmas Eve. (I never understood why they called it midnight Mass when it began at 10:00 p.m. and was over by 11:00 p.m.)

In 1975 I was sixteen years old and a high school junior at Jackson Preparatory School. The institution was private and exclusive and certainly not Christian. So my irreligious profile made no difference. At that time Jackson Prep was an all-white academic and athletic powerhouse, cranking out future Division 1 college athletes, debutantes, doctors, frat boys, and socialites. I was none of the above, except white. My dad was in the liquor business. Because he was the marketing representative for twenty-eight brands, I had access to advertising paraphernalia such as T-shirts, jackets, golf balls, and every branded promotional piece imaginable. These were warehoused in our garage.

Instead of wearing monogrammed sweaters and designer shirts branded with little alligators and polo players as all my friends at Jackson Prep did, my wardrobe consisted of blue jeans and liquor gear: Bacardi Rum golf shirt on Monday, Harvey Wallbanger T-shirt on Tuesday, J&B jacket on Wednesday, and so on.

In 1976, my sophomore year, First Presbyterian Church (First Pres) hired an enthusiastic new graduate from Reformed Theological Seminary as their youth pastor. The ink on Ron Musselman's diploma was not completely dry when he arrived at one of the more affluent churches in Jackson. Each Sunday morning the parking lot at First Pres was littered with the same German sedans and American sports cars that filled the prep school parking lot during the week.

Ron didn't really look like the typical prep guy. When long

hair was the trend, he had short hair, plus he always carried a Bible that he somehow managed to stuff into his back pocket. Lucky for us, Ron didn't really know what he was supposed to be doing. Instead of sitting in the youth pastor's office planning social activities for the First Pres teens, he made it his mission to go out and find some really lost kids. Ron left the ninety-nine and went after the one.

And so it was that Ron Musselman, certified master of theology and upstart youth pastor, came to my high school. He seemed to show up at every school event. It was as if he appointed himself unofficial chaplain of our football team, baseball team, basketball team, track team, and any other group he could identify. Ron was everywhere.

This youth pastor did not wait for people like me to come to his youth group. He took the youth group to us. A couple days each week there would be a table in the lunchroom where Ron held his little Bible study with a few students. My buddies and I would buy boxes of Milk Duds candy, strategically position ourselves in the cafeteria, and toss Milk Duds at the Bible study group. Every now and then we would throw M&M's, but Milk Duds were bigger and had a greater impact. This was my first involvement with small group discipleship. Had I known that in biblical history there was a long tradition of persecuting people by throwing things at them (usually stones), it would have added to my enthusiasm.

Ron left the ninety-nine
and went after the one.

An unintended consequence of all this fun was that eventually Ron figured out where the Milk Duds were coming from. We then became his high-priority prayer target. I ran for six months as the short-haired Jesus guy with the Bible relentlessly pursued me. Finally, concluding that he was never going to give up, I prayed his prayer, thinking he would then leave me alone. It only got worse after that. We met regularly in what he called an action group. I did not know what to call it at the time, but Ron had begun discipling my friends and me. Just like the team of Americans who came to Manila in 1984, Ron knew that he had very little time. By the time I surrendered my life to Christ, I was in the middle of my junior year in high school. So whatever he could do to establish me in the faith and equip me to minister to others had to be done in the next eighteen months. It was intense discipleship.

MEANWHILE, BACK AT HOME

My mom was happy about my newfound faith, but my dad—that was a different story. About the same time I surrendered to Ron (or Jesus), my older brother Jim had had his own life-changing encounter with the Lord. I remember Jim coming home from college for the weekend. We all sat down for dinner, but before we could dive into our food, Jim insisted that we thank God for the meal. We all just froze. That had never happened at our house before except maybe on Thanksgiving Day.

Jim began to passionately pray like a veteran preacher. The prayer continued for what seemed like an eternity. At one point in the extended blessing, Jim prayed, "Lord, we know that You said in the Book of Deuteronomy..." At that point in my brief spiritual journey, I had never heard of Deuteronomy. My head was bowed and my eyes shut tight. I was too afraid to look up. I was thinking that Jim ought to stop but was more than a little apprehensive about what would happen when he did.

True to form, Ron's spiritual radar began to turn toward my dad. My father became a high priority on Ron's prayer list, and he insisted that I regularly pray for him too. He would ask me about my dad every time he saw me. Was I praying for him? Had I been honoring him? Almost every time I met with Ron, we prayed for my dad. Every chance he got, Ron spent time talking with my dad, trying to help him understand the gospel. Eventually my dad received Christ by faith, but that would be decades later.

Every week my friends and I would go to Ron's Tuesday night youth Bible study along with a couple hundred other high school kids. We were learning God's Word, and our friends were getting saved. In time, hundreds in my high school came to Christ. Almost all those new believers were the result of small group discipleship, not big meetings. The emphasis was on establishing theological foundations, practically following Christ, and sharing the gospel with our friends.

A couple of times I attended First Presbyterian on Sunday, but the experience left me completely bored. Nothing about those Sunday morning worship services related to me. It was hard to identify with what they were talking about, and I certainly looked out of place in my jeans and Chuck Taylor All-Stars amid a sea of dark suits. Fortunately, Ron was a lot like Jesus in that he enthusiastically welcomed and pursued people like me. I am thankful that Ron's only concern was my spiritual growth, not the growth of First Pres. He never seemed concerned that I did not become a regular church member.

My First Experience With Spiritual Power

My brother found this place called Bethel House of God on the other side of the tracks. (This is not to be confused with the Bethel World Outreach Center, an Every Nation church in Nashville.) Our peaceful suburban neighborhood was a long way geographically and culturally from that part of town. I never knew that places like that existed in Jackson.

It wasn't long before my friend Greg Ball and I began going to Bethel on Saturday nights. We would drive down there in Greg's dad's Lincoln Town Car and park right out front. Both of us were pretty naïve about the safety of the car and never wondered why no other cars were parked on the street. Looking back, I am amazed that the wheels were still on when we came out. I suppose people thought that such a car must have been the property of a big-time drug dealer, and so they left it alone.

Despite the neighborhood, I felt safe with Greg. He was a black belt in karate and a full-contact kickboxer, the precursor to MMA (mixed martial arts). I had read in the Bible about angels protecting people. I had some measure of faith in those angels but figured that if the angel thing did not work out, Greg had my back.

Bethel House of God met in this little, dilapidated shack. I think some people lived at Bethel, or at least they slept there.

There were all kinds of interesting people there—not really the prep school and First Presbyterian types. It was a combo boarding house, rehabilitation facility, and revival center. There were few chairs. Most people just sat on the floor, stood on the stairway, or found any open space they could. When it rained, there was a pot on the piano to catch the water.

Greg and I thought it was the greatest place ever because we never knew what would happen next. Every time we went, people would be dramatically saved, healed, or delivered. Sometimes the meeting would go past midnight. We would see undeniable miracles and exorcisms right before our eyes. One cold winter night this huge dude with a twelve-inch beard and no shirt kicked the door down, burst in swinging an axe, and began cursing the preacher. Two huge scary-looking Bethel "ushers," or bouncers, threw him out and told him not to come back until he wanted to get right with God. Wow! What a way to spend Saturday night!

Occasionally Greg and I would bring our prep school and First Pres friends to Bethel. It was definitely a change of pace spiritually. For some reason, few ever came back. However, Greg and I kept going. It was better than any action-adventure movie we had ever seen.

Little did I know that two foundational building blocks were being established in my Christian life. In time, both would become key ingredients in the Victory–Manila recipe. The power and the presence of the Holy Spirit, which I learned at Bethel, combined with Christ-centered, Word-based, systematic small group discipleship I received at First Presbyterian would become two nonnegotiable Victory essentials. I'm thankful that God sovereignly saved me through a

Presbyterian church, then added a Spirit-empowered charismatic experience on top of a thoroughly biblical foundation.

A Rope of Sand

When I first moved to the Philippines, I contacted several of the pastors of the largest churches in Manila to ask for a few minutes of their time. I wanted to know how they were able to reach so many people. I was in my early twenties with a church of less than two hundred. They led congregations of multiple thousands. I was desperate to learn. I was lucky when a few of them actually agreed to meet with me and answer my questions. I'll never forget what one pastor told me: "Revival will get people in your church, but it takes administration to keep them in your church. A move of the Holy Spirit will attract people. But if you don't learn how to administrate, organize, and build systems, the revival will be short-lived."

That is truly the history of great revival movements. Few have ever been able to maintain the spiritual momentum for very long, much less transfer it from one generation to the next. George Whitefield was Methodism's first and most popular spokesman. Why is it then that the movement he co-led with John Wesley is known as the Wesleyan Revival and not the Whitefield Revival? Adam Clarke, an early historian of Methodism, suggests the reason was that John Wesley formed small groups for discipleship while Whitefield did not. Clarke writes, "We [Methodists] have been enabled to establish permanent and holy churches over the world. Mr. Wesley saw the necessity of this from the beginning. Mr. Whitefield, when he separated from Mr. Wesley, did not follow it. What was the consequence? The fruit of Mr. Whitefield's labour died with himself. Mr. Wesley's remains and multiplies."[1]

John Wesley was a great administrator and extremely methodical in everything he did. You might say that between Wesley and Whitefield, Wesley was the linear thinker. That was especially true in the way he made disciples. The Wesleyan movement was called Methodism because of its methodical approach to the discipleship process.

The two great revivalists eventually split over doctrinal issues (Calvinism versus Arminianism) and carried on separately. Whitefield, the extraordinary evangelist, did not continue with John Wesley's small group discipleship model. Later in his life Whitefield realized his mistake, as historian Adam Clarke records through a conversation Whitefield had with an old friend, John Poole. Whitefield told his friend:

> John, thou art in thy right place. My brother Wesley acted wisely: the souls that were awakened under his ministry he joined in class [small groups or classes], and thus preserved the fruits of his labour. This I neglected, and my people are a rope of sand.[2]

Looking back on my early days as a Christian, Ron Musselman's discipleship groups were structured and sometimes boring. We were always memorizing Scripture and praying together for our lost friends. At Bethel we saw demonstrations of the power of God that would make the hair on the back of our necks stand up. A few years later I began to check up on all my old friends from high school. To my knowledge three or four Bethelites ended up in the ministry. However, from my graduating class alone at Jackson Prep, there were at that time more than twenty people in full-time ministry as a result of those small, "boring" discipleship groups.

From 1991 to 1993 we were struggling with our new Shangri-La church plant full of people we had not won to Christ, and I wondered why it wasn't fun anymore. I thought back to my early Christian experiences. I always had—and still do desire—to embrace the power of God and the presence of the Holy Spirit. I determined, however, that if I accomplished nothing else, Victory–Manila was going to be about making disciples. It was at that point in the history of our church that we made a commitment to create a relational culture and to implement a discipleship strategy that would be our one unstoppable spiritual judo move.

COPYING METHODS
OR CATCHING THE SPIRIT

I can understand why a leader would say, "Let's not try to reinvent the wheel. Let's find what is working and duplicate it in our church." However, a process works because it fits the culture you are trying to engage, the leadership team trying to implement it, and the people who are going to execute it.

On numerous occasions I have had people from the United States approach me to deliver their happy news—that they are doing small group discipleship in their church exactly the way we do it in the Philippines. Instead of the expected congratulations and a pat on the back, my typical response is, "Why in the world would you do that?" I will give them this explanation: "I'm in a city of twelve million people. Most of them live in poverty, very few young people have cars, it is an animistic

Catholic culture, and the family structure is totally different from that in the West. The world you live in is completely different from Manila. Why would you copy us?"

When I was just starting out in ministry back in the late 1970s and early 1980s, the greatest spiritual awakening and the world's fastest-growing church was in Seoul, South Korea. David Yonggi Cho had thousands of small groups, a mountain with hundreds of prayer caves dug into the side of it, and half a million people attending his church. Christian leaders and church growth experts flocked to Korea to study his model and bring it back to the United States. One US church acquired its own prayer mountain, but I don't know whether they got around to digging out the little caves. It is great to learn from others, but South Korea is not at all like the United States. Korean culture is very traditional, inflexible, and top-down. Americans are, by contrast, far more independent and innovative and do not like being told what to do. You do not hear much about the Korean model anymore in America because over the long haul it simply did not work.

The world you live in is
completely different from Manila.
Why would you copy us?

Rick Warren has developed a tremendous church growth model that has indeed worked in an American city. Many have read his books and tried to implement Saddleback's purpose-driven model in their own churches. What they failed to take into consideration was that Saddleback Community Church is located in one of the wealthiest and most educated counties in the United States. Rick cracked the missional code for his community, but the code is different in every community.

There was a big purpose-driven campaign in Manila a few years ago, inspired by Rick's best-selling book *The Purpose-Driven Life*. The long-term impact on church growth in the Philippines was minimal because poor people are just not all that interested in purpose. They are more concerned about their next meal. However, our church took advantage of all the purpose-driven publicity by conducting a campaign, but first rewriting all the materials to address Filipino needs in Manila. At Victory the campaign was a phenomenal success because, rather than copying what worked in California, we changed it to engage Filipino culture and community.

A few years ago people started flocking to Bogotá, Colombia, to learn about the G-12 (groups of twelve) cell group strategy employed by César Castellanos and his 100,000-member church. We sent a couple of Victory pastors, Ferdie Cabiling and Dennis Sy, to study the Bogotá model for a few weeks and to borrow some ideas. Ferdie came home with this summary report: "The secret to their growth is not their system. In fact, I think ours is better. The secret to their power is their compassion for the lost. Any church that loves and prays for lost people like those Bogotá people will grow no matter what discipleship system they use." So, rather than copying their program, their vocabulary, or their system, we tried to catch their spirit—their love for the lost.

Various aspects of what we do will work for you, others can be adapted to fit your culture, and some parts should be completely replaced by your own inventions. You have to formulate a system that is appropriate for your cultural setting. There are even areas of Manila where pastors are modifying our process to adapt to the ethnic demographics of their communities. Writing your own program for making disciples takes time, prayer, and some trial and error—just as it did with us. We can, however, learn from one another, just as the Victory team is continuing to learn and incorporate ideas from other churches around the world, but only after modification to make sure the strategies make sense in our culture and community.

The Starting Point

Church leaders frequently ask me to evaluate their new or improved process of making disciples. They want to know whether I think a particular process will work in their church. While I have a pretty good sense of what will and will not work in Manila, the culture is changing so quickly that staying relevant requires our constant attention. If we allow ourselves to be distracted by focusing on the mechanics of our own efforts rather than our culture, we will become irrelevant almost overnight.

So when someone asks for my opinion about their disciple-making process, the first thought that comes to mind is, *What makes you think I am going to know?* Because, however, that is not a very good answer to a sincere question, my more thoughtful response addresses three concerns:

1. Lead by example.

Change is difficult. In many cases we come to the conclusion that we have to make a change only after the situation has become desperate. That was certainly the case for us in the early nineties. Significant difficulties were what caused us to make equally significant changes in the way we did things. But *how* you make the change can be as important as *what* you change. Unfortunately, three questions that often emerge in discussions about adopting a new process of making disciples are: (1) How much will it cost? (2) How easily can it be implemented? and (3) How soon will we begin to see results? If those are the chief concerns that are driving the approach to a new process, you might be headed for more problems than solutions.

Values clarification is a good place to start. Does your team have a clear and commonly shared understanding of what it means to be a disciple of Jesus? In other words, precisely what does it mean to follow Jesus, fish for men, and fellowship with others? How about those three key relationships—with Jesus, with nonbelievers, and with believers?

The leaders with the greatest effectiveness lead from the front, not from the rear. That is to say, they do not simply command the action of others as they observe from a safe distance. They continually lead by example and by challenging others to follow. Translating that into church-change language, we should not try to change the church without first changing ourselves. I cannot reasonably hope for members at Victory–Manila to adopt a lifestyle of honoring God and making disciples if I am not doing it myself. There are many layers of leadership between the first-time small group leader and myself. Yet Deborah and I, along with the rest of the leadership team, can never graduate from making disciples just as the newest members do.

Live it before you teach it.

To lead by example means that we get our own minds and hearts focused on making disciples before trying to organize others to do so. Set your mind on following Jesus, fishing for men, and fellowshiping with others. More fundamentally, set your heart on deepening your relationship with Jesus, your relationship with nonbelievers, and your relationship with other disciples who are trying to do the same thing. In other words, live it before you teach it.

2. Nothing works without commitment and consistency.

What I mean is that no discipleship process works automatically apart from our own commitment to make it work. Even the best church growth models can actually weaken or even destroy churches if implemented without a high level of commitment to see them through. Repeatedly starting and abandoning new programs in a church causes the leadership to lose credibility. After numerous ideas are introduced and subsequently discarded, people are far more likely to sit back and roll their eyes with a wait-and-see attitude when the next idea is presented. With each round it becomes more and more difficult to inspire people, mobilize them to action, or simply get them to buy into anything you want to do.

One of my typical comments to leaders formulating their own process of making disciples is that the details of their system are not as important as how committed they are to the process. Even if you had the perfect disciple-making process for your community, it would not work automatically without commitment and consistency.

We have been updating and adjusting our methods for decades, not because we had nothing better to do, but always because some aspect of our process was not working as well as it should. Even though we have gained momentum through the years with the Victory discipleship process, it does not fuel itself. Focused hard work is required to keep it running.

What enables us to keep putting in the effort, fixing the problems, and seeking God about how to do it better? It is that we have committed ourselves to making disciples. We are not committed to getting big or to staying small. We are not committed to reaching politicians, athletes, or actors— rich people, poor people, or smart people. We are not committed to prosperity, political influence, popularity, or fame. We did not set out to formulate and implement a discipleship strategy to see whether it would work. What keeps us at it is not merely a *long-term* commitment but a *lifetime* commitment to the Great Commission. We are here to honor God and make disciples. We have no plan B.

3. Integrate everything around your primary objective.

Some churches have dozens of programs designed to address every demographic and every imaginable need. In fact, a church's effectiveness is often measured by the number of programs they have—a good church will have a dozen programs, a great church will have twenty, and a super church will have a hundred.

At Victory–Manila we have one program with four distinct elements that we have been modifying and perfecting for many years. What makes the process successful is that each element is integrated with the others and aimed at a single target— making disciples who make other disciples. Our process of engaging culture through small groups feeds our process of establishing spiritual foundations through Victory Weekends. Young believers who have completed a Victory Weekend populate the Making Disciples and Training for Victory classes, which equip relatively new believers to serve as small group leaders. Graduates are immediately empowered to establish their own small groups to engage nonbelievers for Christ. And the cycle begins all over again.

As we have become more effective at each of those elements of our discipleship process, the process has gradually gained more and more momentum. It began as a slow but sure movement of making disciples. Today it is more like a gigantic boulder rolling down a hill. One generation of disciples creates a larger generation of disciples that in turn creates another still larger generation of disciples, and so on. It is the kind of multiplication that can get wonderfully out of control.

That is precisely what started happening to us around 1991 and 1992. For the first six years, we made some disciples and *added* a lot of people to the church. Attendance went from 165 to 2,000. The key word I used to describe that first stage of growth at Victory is *added*. At that time it was an addition process, and I worked very hard adding people while at the same time working equally hard trying to keep from subtracting (or losing) people. The key word in this description is *I*. I worked at it so hard that the process began destroying my health. We changed our process of making disciples in the early nineties to one that caused us to grow by multiplication rather than addition. The key to moving forward successfully was a commonly shared idea about the definition of discipleship, a single focus, and a process-with-program element that worked together, not independently.

THE IMPORTANCE OF CLARITY AND DEFINITION

In the first few chapters of this book I talked briefly about the history, the philosophy, the goals, and the results of what we do at Victory. I used words such as *principles, process, methods,* and *models* interchangeably. Inside our leadership team discussions we tend to define things a bit more precisely, especially the following words and concepts.

Discipleship principles. We have identified four principles that serve as the foundation of what we believe and practice about discipleship. These principles are not unique to our context, but, like all principles, they are true for all time and in all places. Some people use different words and phrases, but the principles are the same. All four are essential. If one is removed, the discipleship process breaks down. We call these four principles the Four Es—engage, establish, equip, and empower.

Church culture. As we live out our values over time, we create a unique and distinct culture—mostly for better but sometimes for worse. While it is easy to rebrand and rewrite value and vision statements, changing a church's culture is a time-consuming and tedious task. Church culture is developed over time, and it takes time to change it. I have seen many well-meaning church leaders use our discipleship material, copy our Four Es language, and start small group discipleship, only to fail as quickly as they started. Why? Most failed because they planted discipleship principles and ideas into the soil of a culture that killed the seeds. When it comes to making disciples, creating the right culture is much more important than using the right language and material. I wish I could tell you it's easy, but changing and maintaining a healthy discipleship culture is the most difficult and elusive part of ministry.

Discipleship goals. Our ultimate goal is expressed in our Victory motto: Honor God; *make disciples.* This book focuses on one aspect of that goal—how we make disciples. The *honor God* part of the motto is our way of expressing organizational values that describe our relationship with God and with one another. That is an entirely different book. But there are subgoals that flow out of the previously mentioned values, culture, and principles. Identifying these basic discipleship goals helps us hit the big goal of honoring God and making disciples.

Church Culture	Discipleship Principle	Basic Goal
Relational	Engage culture and community	Share the gospel
Spiritual	Establish biblical foundations	Strong foundations
Intentional	Equip believers to minister	Basic ministry skills
Missional	Empower disciples to make disciples	Ministry confidence and competence

WIKICHURCH LESSONS

Everyone wants to make disciples, but many try, fail, then quit. Why? I think the easiest and most common way to fail at discipleship is to import a model or copy a method that worked somewhere else without first understanding the values that create a healthy discipleship culture. Principles and process are much more important than material, models, and methods.

WikiChurches create an ongoing process of making disciples who in turn make other disciples. This takes time, effort, and persistence. Among the reasons we have been successful are:

1. We took the time as a leadership team to fine-tune our common understanding of what it means to be a disciple.

2. We did not make sudden, radical changes in the church. Discipleship groups designed to engage nonbelievers began with the leadership team and slowly grew from there.

3. We made the decision to perfect one move (making disciples) rather than dozens of independent programs.

None of those steps are necessarily easy, but they are not complicated either. Perhaps the most difficult part for some is a simple decision—to progressively move the church toward the single focus of making disciples.

CHAPTER FIVE

CATCHING BIRDS, FISHING FOR MEN, AND ASHTRAY EVANGELISM

IT WAS ABOUT thirteen years ago, and I was making a routine call home to talk to my wife. I expected her to answer the phone but was surprised to hear the voice of my seven-year-old saying, "Hello, this is Jonathan." That greeting was music to my ears! We had been working on Jonathan's phone etiquette. He usually answered something like, "Who is this, and what do you want?" Progress at last!

"Hey, Jonathan. This is Dad. You're home from school early. What are you doing?"

"I'm catchin' birds."

"Catching birds?" I was curious. "And just how are you doing that?"

"It's easy, Dad. I got this box and turned it upside down and used a chopstick to hold it up and put breadcrumbs under the box and tied dental floss to the chopstick. Then I hide under the table and when birds go under the box to eat the bread, I pull the dental floss, and the box falls on the birds, and I catch 'em and make 'em pet birds."

"How many have you caught so far?"

"None yet."

I didn't have the heart to tell Jonathan that it probably wouldn't work. He would find that out soon enough; then he'd get busy figuring out a way to make our car fly or something like that. He's always been our creative one.

Vivid thirty-year-old memories of my brother and me making our own bird trap flooded my mind that day. I remembered the excitement when we came up with the idea. I remembered the frustration when all the birds seemed to suddenly migrate to Canada as soon as we finished our trap. No, not a single bird was left in the whole state of Mississippi. At least that's the way it seemed, because if any birds were still in the state, we would have caught them.

"Catchin' Fish"

Eventually I got my wife on the phone, forgot why I called, and ended up telling her the bird story. We shared a good laugh, and I went back to my work. But I could not stop thinking about my son's futile attempt at catching birds. It reminded me too much of church.

While almost every preteen boy on the planet has made a bird trap, I have never met one who actually caught a bird in a box. It's a great idea with just one problem: it doesn't work. But the fact that no one (except Bear Grylls from *Man vs. Wild*) has caught a bird with a box, a stick, and a string since the Jurassic period has not stopped each new generation from trying. Again, it reminds me of church.

"Hello, this is Pastor Joe."

"Hey, Pastor Joe. What are you doing?"

"Fishin' for men."

"How many you caught so far?"

"None yet. In fact, our church hasn't caught any this decade, but we are still using the same methods that every generation has used for the past hundred years. We've got a signboard with the sermon title out front, and there's pizza and a quartet to entertain the youth in the basement. So it is just a matter of time before the fish start jumping into our boat. I can feel it. We're on the verge of a great revival!"

If we are serious about engaging our culture and communities today, then it is about time we throw away our box, stick, and string methods and learn to engage our communities and our culture. The church has invented, packaged, branded, and marketed countless versions of the box, stick, and string. That's all great except for the fact that these tired methods are causing all the "fish" to swim away.

We may not be called to catch birds, but we are called to fish for people. So the questions are: How to do we catch people? How do we engage our communities and connect with our culture? Or maybe we should just continue with the church version of the box, stick, and string.

"A Friend of Sinners"

Growing up I was not too interested in church or religion. When I became a teenager, a few times I was invited by Christian classmates to attend their church youth group activities and Bible studies. I was pretty good at saying no. I was not ready to dive into their world; however, I couldn't keep them from diving into mine. I am forever grateful that Ron Musselman, the First Pres youth pastor, did not just invite me to his church world; he jumped into my not-so-churchy world. Because I was not interested in engaging religious culture and church community, Ron engaged my culture and my community.

Jesus gave the greatest demonstration of engaging culture and community when He left the streets of gold in heaven to walk the dirt roads of the Roman Empire. He left his throne to be born in a barn. He left heaven to come to Earth. Showing up on Earth was just the beginning. While here, He was the expert at engaging all types of cultures and communities that were traditionally disenfranchised by the religious elite.

Two thousand years ago some people liked Jesus, and others hated Him. Some enjoyed His company; others avoided Him like the plague. Some were attracted to Him; others were offended by Him. Think for a moment: who was attracted to Jesus? Who liked to hang around Him? I can think of two types of people who were attracted to Jesus: children and "sinners." In fact, it seems that the more youthful and the more sinful, the more they were attracted to Him.

One time when little children started crowding around

Jesus, His followers got in the way, thinking that Jesus ν "adults only" kind of person. Mark records that "when Jesus saw this, he was indignant" (Mark 10:14). Warning: When church people act as if Jesus is only interested in old people, watch out, because this really ticks Him off.

It was not only the youth who were attracted to Jesus, but also those who seemed the furthest from God. Most Christians attend too many prayer meetings and Bible studies to ever meet an authentic, card-carrying, nonreligious sinner. Furthermore, the few Christians who actually meet a "sinner" or two don't really like them. The strange colors in their hair, the holes in their ears, the ink art on their skin, and the cigarettes in their mouths are offensive to the average Christianese-speaking church person.

Jesus was able to engage His culture and relate to His generation because He was not afraid that contact with non-believers would tarnish His holiness. Rather, He knew that His holiness would cleanse their filth. He was relevant because He walked where they walked, but He did not do what they did. He spent time with drunkards but never got drunk. He ate with corrupt tax officials, but He was not corrupt. He extended compassion to prostitutes but never compromised His moral standards.

Jesus was called "a friend of sinners" because He deliberately spent time with religious outsiders. We are irrelevant to our sinful generation because we spend too much time around Christians and not enough time around the unchurched. Jesus engaged their world. We invite them to our church meetings.

Now, think about who did not enjoy Jesus's company. Who hated Him? Who couldn't stand to be around Him? As hard as it is for church people to grasp, the fact is that the more religious the person, the more he hated Jesus and everything He stood for.

Youth and sinners liked Him; religious people hated Him. How opposite it is today. Who is repelled by church? Who gets dragged to church against their will? Who finds church painfully boring and irrelevant? You guessed it: sinners and young people. On the other hand, who loves church activity, church music, and Christian TV? Right again: religious people.

Isn't it strange that religious people hated Jesus, but two thousand years later they love church? And isn't it strange that youth and sinners were originally attracted to Jesus, but today they are repelled by church? That's the difference between engaging their world and inviting them to engage ours but then judging them when they don't. If we are to follow in Jesus's footsteps, engage our culture and communities, and live life as "friends of sinners," then we need to know what real friendship is.

THE POWER OF
AUTHENTIC FRIENDSHIP

Jackie Robinson, the first black man to play professional Major League Baseball in the United States, has become an international sports icon. He is recognized as one of the all-time best to ever play America's favorite sport. He was not always held in such high regard. If not for an unexpected act of friendship, his career could have ended the same year it started.

Jackie broke into Major League Baseball during a time of racial prejudice, strife, and violence. He was a black man entering a white man's world. Fans, umpires, opposing players, and sometimes even his own teammates went out of their way to let him know he did not belong in their league. A low moment came during a road game in Cincinnati when the crowd, reacting to the unusual presence of black fans in the stands, was particularly cruel. They shouted all manner of racial insults at Jackie, worse than any he had heard since he joined the Brooklyn Dodgers.[1]

Jackie took his position at first base for what seemed like an eternity as the vicious fans continued to voice their disapproval. Then Pee Wee Reese, the white shortstop, walked across the infield and stood next to Jackie. With his arm around Jackie's shoulder, Pee Wee began talking in Jackie's ear. Years later, neither man would recall what Pee Wee said. It didn't matter. His actions spoke loud and clear. The longer this white man stood shoulder to shoulder with his black teammate and friend, the quieter the crowd got until there was a deafening silence.[2] Jackie later said Pee Wee's demonstration of friendship that day not only silenced the crowd, but it also helped break down the racial tension within the team that threatened to end his career.[3]

It is amazing what sincere friendship can accomplish. Jesus extended friendship to people who had been rejected, judged, and marginalized by religious leaders and religious institutions. What do you think could happen if we extend friendship to the nonreligious, unchurched people in our communities? What if we become the kind of "friend who sticks closer than a brother," not just to church people but to the unchurched as well? Engaging culture and community is all about building bridges of friendship, not religious walls.

Lost and Found

The Gospel of Luke records the story of three lost things—the lost sheep, the lost coin, and the lost son. The context or background of this passage is as important as the story itself. The three stories are Jesus's response to an accusation or a "mutter" by some religious leaders.

> Now the tax collectors and "sinners" were all gathering around to hear him. But the Pharisees and the teachers of the law muttered, "This man welcomes sinners and eats with them."
>
> —Luke 15:1–2

As usual, the nonreligious were hanging around Jesus, and the super-religious were judging and complaining. The religious leaders and theological experts had been following Jesus for several years, watching and waiting for Him to violate some rule or tradition, which they would then use as the basis for an indictment against Him. They watched Him every day—everywhere He went, everything He did, everything He said. No wonder Jesus frequently took His disciples away to a lonely place. I can imagine the fingers being pointed at Jesus as the religious leaders angrily pronounced their indictment.

"This man welcomes sinners!" the lead investigator growls. All his fellow spies nod their heads, moaning to show their self-righteous disgust. "And He eats with them!" the investigator shouts, and the rest of Jesus's accusers raise their voices in a show of anger and condemnation.

Without going into a long discussion of Pharisaic traditions, I will simply say that Pharisees were aggressively evangelistic.

One of their goals was to convert and disciple heathen. On one occasion Jesus denounced the hypocrisy of the Pharisees with these words:

> Woe to you, teachers of the law and Pharisees, you hypocrites! You travel over land and sea to win a single convert, and when he becomes one, you make him twice as much a son of hell as you are.
>
> —MATTHEW 23:15

Though tax collectors and others who had collaborated with the Roman occupiers might have been outside the realm of potential converts, the Pharisees did indeed admit sinners. Those who were desperate enough to join their group were allowed to become proselytes to Judaism. But the Pharisees certainly made no efforts to personally engage nonbelievers where they were. Quite the contrary, the Pharisees identified themselves in terms of non-engagement. As a result, the accusation against Jesus was that He not only welcomed sinners, but He also ate with them. In other words, He fellowshiped, shared His life, and hung out with sinners. In another passage, Jesus summarized the indictment against Him this way:

> For John the Baptist came neither eating bread nor drinking wine, and you say, "He has a demon." The Son of Man came eating and drinking, and you say, "Here is a glutton and a drunkard, a friend of tax collectors and 'sinners.'"
>
> —LUKE 7:33–35

The religious leaders defined their righteousness and their mission in terms of non-engagement; Jesus did the exact opposite. He defined righteousness and mission in terms of engagement with those who, in one way or another, were lost. He said of Himself: "For the Son of Man came to seek and to save what was lost" (Luke 19:10).

Now, if those same Pharisees sent an investigative team to follow you and me around every day, what would their conclusion be? Would they accuse us of being like Jesus, or would they say something like this: "We've been watching your life—church on Sunday, Bible study on Tuesday, prayer meeting on Wednesday, coffee with church members on Thursday, choir practice on the weekend. We have concluded that without a doubt that you are a *friend of Christians*." When is the last time you had dinner with nonbelievers? Where are the intentional nonchurch friendships? If we are really following Jesus, if we are really striving to be like Him, then where are the lost people in our lives?

STRINGS
DEFINITELY ATTACHED

There is a lot of talk today about performing acts of kindness without any strings attached. That is certainly better than no kindness or no engagement at all with nonbelievers. However, I am pretty sure that ministry without message was not the way Jesus or the apostle Paul approached it. Paul wrote to the Corinthian church:

> Though I am free and belong to no man, I make myself a slave to everyone, *to win as many as possible*. To the Jews I became like a Jew, *to win the Jews*. To those under the law I became like one under the

law (though I myself am not under the law), so as *to win those under the law.* To those not having the law I became like one not having the law (though I am not free from God's law but am under Christ's law), so as *to win those not having the law.* To the weak I became weak, to win the weak. I have become all things to all men so that by all possible means I might save some. I do all this *for the sake of the gospel,* that I may share in its blessings.

—1 Corinthians 9:19–23,
EMPHASIS ADDED

The apostle Paul was saying that he went to great lengths to engage all kinds of nonbelievers. To those under the law, he became like one under the law. To the weak, he became weak. In other words, he worked hard at identifying and building common ground with people. Paul, however, was no undercover Christian, and there was no mystery about his motivations. He clearly had strings attached, his goal being to win as many people to Christ as he could.

*Are we truly
friends of sinners?*

Although Jesus constantly engaged people at every level of society and spirituality, there is no example in the gospels that could come close to implying that He was anything but straightforward about the righteousness, repentance, and kingdom to which He called them. God is full of mercy and kindness, but the kindness of God toward nonbelievers or toward those living in sin is for one purpose. As Paul wrote in Romans 2:4, "Do you show contempt for the riches of his kindness, tolerance and patience, not realizing that *God's kindness leads you toward repentance?*" (emphasis added). As Jesus's followers, if we are really striving to be like Him, there are actually two questions we should ask ourselves.

The first is, Are we truly friends of sinners? And the second is, Are our nonbelieving friends being compelled to become Christ's followers through their relationship with us? The context of Luke 15 is Jesus's explanation to those who accused Him of welcoming and eating with tax collectors and sinners. He responded to them with three parables. The first one is about a shepherd with one hundred sheep. One sheep is lost, so the shepherd leaves the ninety-nine and goes after the lost one until he finds it. Then he returns and with joy tells all his friends he has found his lost sheep. The second story is about a woman who lost a coin. She searches for it until she finds it, then tells her friends and neighbors to rejoice with her. After these two stories, Jesus said, "In the same way, I tell you, there is rejoicing in the presence of the angels of God over one sinner who repents" (Luke 15:10).

THE NINETY-NINE
AND THE ONE

In the story of the lost sheep, Jesus asked, "Does he [the shepherd] not leave the ninety-nine to go after the missing one?" In modern-day motivational language, we would phrase the question like this: "Is the glass 99 percent full or 1 percent empty?" While we immediately assume that "99 percent full" is the right answer, apparently Jesus seemed to focus more on the missing one.

The shepherd in Luke 15 intentionally devoted himself to pursuing what was lost. He left all the non-lost sheep exposed "in the open country." No matter how many ways you look at this account, there is always an aspect of it that betrays common sense. Why jeopardize the ninety-nine in an effort to search for the one? How does that build the herd? How does it accomplish the greater good?

The third parable is about a father and two sons. His younger son is lost. The older son has serious attitude issues. This third story presents yet another response that seems to fly in the face of conventional wisdom. When the lost son returns, the father is so overjoyed that he kills the fatted calf and has a great celebration. The non-lost son was furious and refused to rejoice with the father, saying:

> "Look! All these years I've been slaving for you and never disobeyed your orders. Yet you never gave me even a young goat so I could celebrate with my friends. But when this son of yours who has squandered your property with prostitutes comes home, you kill the fattened calf for him!"
>
> "My son," the father said, "you are always with me, and everything I have is yours. But we had to celebrate and be glad, because this brother of yours was dead and is alive again; he was lost and is found."
>
> —LUKE 15:29–32

The older brother seems to have a good point, doesn't he? Why pay so much attention and spend so much money on those who rejected and dishonored you rather than on those who are and have been following you? To put it in a more contemporary way, why focus so much of our attention on pursuing those who are lost when those in the church have so many needs of their own? If we do not focus our attention on our members, will they not go somewhere else? Will we not lose the ninety-nine as we are off pursuing the one? Jesus defended the pursuit of the coin and the one lost sheep by saying there will be more rejoicing in heaven over one sinner who repents than over ninety-nine righteous persons who do not need to repent. Obviously, you get a very different perspective on things as they are viewed from heaven.

In light of the radical idea of leaving ninety-nine and going after one, we have to repeatedly ask ourselves the obvious question: Considering the total expenditure of money, time, and effort from staff and volunteers, how does the church commit to finding the lost one as compared to serving the ninety-nine found? As it is sometimes said, the church is an organization that exists for its nonmembers. This is why our leadership team made the radical decision in the early nineties to organize Victory for the twenty thousand we had not yet reached rather than for the two thousand we had already reached. That was our way of saying we were leaving the ninety-nine and going after the one.

Jesus did not expect people, especially nonbelievers, to jump into His world, so He jumped into theirs. He was constantly engaging all types of people—Jews and Gentiles, the super-religious and the super sinners, the sincere and self-righteous, the fabulously rich and the desperately poor, Zionist zealots and tax collectors who collaborated with the Roman occupiers. He employed no single method or approach. Each group was different, and even as He engaged individuals within each of those groups, there was no automatic go-to method.

Church leaders in the provinces of the Philippines will engage their culture and community differently than we do in Manila. Even within metro Manila there are areas that have modified or come up with completely different methods of engaging. You can imagine how different the methods must be for China, Mongolia, Laos, or Dubai. Even in the United States there are differences, for example, engaging the community in New York as compared to Nashville, Tennessee. But no matter how diverse or difficult your cultural setting, the biblical principle of engaging culture and community applies to every church in every culture in every era. I cannot tell you the best way to engage your culture and your community, but I can tell you that engaging is the starting point in the disciple-making process.

ASHTRAY EVANGELISM

How far out of your cultural comfort zone are you willing to go in order to engage your culture and community? My American friends Chuck and Sherry Quinley came to the Philippines a few years after we did. Unlike us, they actually had some missionary training and cross-cultural experience, having served in Jamaica. Chuck's day job included everything that goes with being the president of a theological seminary. His Asian Seminary for Christian Ministry specialized in training Asians to reach Asia. He and Sherry did not come to Manila to start a church. The church plant was an accident. It was the unexpected and unavoidable result of engaging their community.

Having moved into a brand-new house, Sherry began to apply her own personal decorating touches, among which were two new sofas and custom-made matching curtains. The living room was where they invited people to come for private meetings, and she wanted that room to be particularly nice.

There was one thing, however, neither of them had taken into consideration, especially when it came to engaging their community. In Asia, thanks to aggressive advertising by tobacco firms, it seems that most people smoke. So, whenever they invited neighbors to their home, their guests would instinctively reach for their pack and light up. About halfway through their cigarettes, it would inevitably become awkward and embarrassing. There were no ashtrays in Chuck and Sherry's home. Their guests would cup their hand apologetically under the drooping ash, and the conversation would stop as they began nervously looking for a solution. Chuck writes:

> To be honest, we didn't want them smoking in our house. We thought they would get the message if there were no ashtrays. We were sacrificing time and energy to get to know them, but there had to be a line drawn somewhere to say, "We will go this far into your world, but no more." Smoking was the line. Smoke made the curtains stink. People burned the new upholstery by carelessly waving their firebrands around.[4]

This went on for a few weeks as Chuck and Sherry continued to rehearse their reasons for no ashtrays. Finally, they began to recognize the Holy Spirit speaking to them, reminding them that people without a relationship with Christ have a big void in their lives and often lack the motivation and the power to quit smoking. Unbelievers already had to overcome numerous obstacles to visit the home of foreign missionaries. The unstated but implied smoking ban had become just one more obstacle between them and Christ. Chuck continues:

> Every husband knows that he is really living in his wife's house. I knew it was up to Sherry to decide and that she had to do it from her heart. One day she came back from the grocery store with an ashtray. I was proud of my wife. The funny thing was that once we had made the decision and purchased the ashtray, hardly anyone ever smoked again in our house.[5]

WikiChurch Lessons

Do you really want to be a WikiChurch? Do you really want to make disciples? Jesus came from heaven to Earth in order to engage our culture and community. Chuck and Sherry bought ashtrays to engage theirs. What about you? Are you willing to go and make disciples, no matter the cost?

The diagram below represents the four aspects of the Wiki-Church discipleship process at Victory–Manila. Once we've engaged our community with the gospel, it is time to start *establishing biblical foundations.*

PRINCIPLE
Engage Culture
and Community

KEY VERSES
Luke 15:1–7
1 Corinthians 9:22

GOAL
Preach the Gospel

CHAPTER SIX

GOOD FAÇADE,
BAD FOUNDATIONS

WHILE CHANGING PLANES in Singapore a few years ago, I noticed a billboard that underscored the importance of foundations. On the sign was a huge picture of the Leaning Tower of Pisa. I'm sure the name of the advertiser was on the sign somewhere—maybe a bank or a car or a hotel. I don't remember. It must not have been a good advertisement since I have no idea what product it was selling. But all these years later, I still remember the tagline under the picture: "Good Façade, Bad Foundations."

Too many Christians are like that leaning tower. They look good on the outside, but because of shallow and weak foundations, they start leaning toward sin as soon as they emerge from the baptism tank. Some are leaning so far that the smallest temptation can potentially knock them down.

Building on
Sinking Sand

Construction on the bell tower in Pisa began in 1173, but there were problems from the beginning. Because of the underground water level in that area, the builders were able to dig the foundation only about ten feet deep—not very deep for an eight-story stone structure.[1]

As the first level of the tower was completed, the south side was already beginning to sink. The builders tried to compensate for the poor foundation by building the columns and arches on the south side about an inch taller than those on the north side. However, by the time they built the fourth floor, they had to add yet another inch to the southern columns, which then became two inches taller than the northern ones. With no apparent fix at hand, construction was halted.[2]

In 1234 the architect Benenato discovered that the tower was leaning even more, which is to say that the foundation continued to sink. Now the south side of the fourth story was a full six inches shorter than the north side. Benenato added a fifth story, increasing the height of the south columns even more, but abandoned the project after adding that one story. After several other starts and stops, two more floors were added.[3]

It takes skill to build a tower straight. It takes an enormous amount of ingenuity to build one straight that started off crooked. Finally, nearly two hundred years after construction began, an ambitious builder completed the top floor with a spiral staircase constructed to compensate for the tilt.[4] By now, the top of the tower was leaning almost five feet.[5]

By the twentieth century, the lean of the Leaning Tower of Pisa had increased to seventeen feet off center at the top, and the tower had to be closed. Eventually a restoration project reinforced the foundation, permanently anchored the tower, and reduced the tilt by fifteen inches—a decade and $27 million for a few inches.[6] Of course, they did not make it perfectly straight because why would people come from around the world to see the Straight Tower of Pisa?

Tragically, many spiritual lives
are built with more concern about
the façade than the foundation.

The builders of the Tower of Pisa did not set out to erect a monument to their own mistakes but a building that would be functional and productive for a long, long time. However, leaning towers are like car wrecks, dysfunctional celebrities, and disgraced politicians. When something goes terribly wrong, people cannot help themselves. They have to stop, look, and maybe take a picture.

Even though the tower began to lean early on in the construction, moving ahead with the project was always more important than fixing the foundation, even when the builders knew it was faulty. They kept trying to make it a functional building by compensating for the fact that it was a house built on sinking sand. Somewhere along the way, Italian architects just gave up and preserved it as a tourist attraction. Good façade, bad foundation. Tragically, many spiritual lives are built with more concern about the façade than the foundation.

FOUNDATIONS FIRST

Foundations are not the most exciting part of a building project, nor are they the most attractive part of the finished building. They are usually ugly and unseen. Yet they are vitally important. Foundations predict the future and determine the ultimate size of the building. The deeper the foundation, the taller the building. The same is true with spiritual foundations. Biblical foundations predict future growth and determine the size and strength of spiritual life.

The dilemma for the many generations of architects who worked on the tower at Pisa was that their foundation was not sufficient to support their mission. The objective was to construct an eight-story bell tower, the highest in all of Europe at the time. I'm sure there was some significance to having the highest tower and loudest bell. But the taller and the heavier that building became, the more the tower leaned. No amount of structural adjustments above the ground could compensate for a shallow foundation on less-than-solid ground. The same is true for individuals and organizations. Nice facilities and flashy programs will not make up for weak foundations.

Many church leaders face the same sort of dilemma as the builders of the tower at Pisa. They know there are serious foundational issues but feel it is too late or too costly to start over. So they focus on the façade, hoping the whole thing does not collapse and take out a bunch of pew-warming tourists. In the meantime they make complicated adjustments to compensate for simple problems in the foundation. That is a picture of where Victory was around 1991. All was well on the surface, but we had some foundational problems regarding the way we were growing. Adopting a new approach was not an easy decision to make. And it was not an easy two years of transition while we changed our culture. But I'm glad we stuck with it.

I wonder how many of the Tower of Pisa architects began with great enthusiasm but then realized the magnitude of the tower's foundational problems and ended up screaming, "Let's just tear it down and start over!" Since that was not an option, they simply quit.

Yes, they did eventually complete the Leaning Tower of Pisa, but the bells had to be removed for fear its weight would topple the building. So it no longer served as a bell tower. It was just a structure with no purpose, one that was slowly falling down. But, hey, it had a really nice façade!

When we constructed the Every Nation building in Manila's Fort Bonifacio, we made it five stories tall at first, but we spent an extra five million pesos on the foundation so we could eventually add three more floors. (The building code for the University Park area of Fort Bonifacio limits buildings to eight stories.) How deeply we dug and how strongly we built at the beginning determined forever how high the building could go.

We spent the extra money on the foundation because we believed that one day we would need to add those three extra floors. Investing heavily in natural and spiritual foundations is an act of faith. We did it naturally, and we do it spiritually because we believe that the foundation not only enables future growth, but it also predicts it and limits it.

In the Sermon on the Mount, Jesus used foundations to show the difference between those who merely claimed to follow Him and those who were truly His disciples.

> Why do you call me, "Lord, Lord," and do not do what I say? I will show you what he is like who comes to me and hears my words and puts them into practice. He is like a man building a house, who *dug down deep and laid the foundation on rock*. When a flood came, the torrent struck that house but could not shake it, because it was well built. But the one who hears my words and does not put them into practice is like a man who built a house on the ground *without a foundation*. The moment the torrent struck that house, it collapsed and its destruction was complete.
>
> —LUKE 6:46–49,
> EMPHASIS ADDED

To apply that passage to the discipleship process, we need to understand the following:

Storms are inevitable.

Jesus invited *anyone* wanting to follow Him to take up his or her cross and come on (Mark 8:34). However, He also warned *everyone* considering the challenge that they needed to count the cost (Luke 14:28). Becoming a disciple of Jesus does not exempt anyone from difficulties in life. Quite the contrary, following Jesus might cause the storms to become more frequent and more intense. It is important for new believers to understand that.

When a watch claims to be waterproof, that does not mean the watch will not get wet. It means that water will not stop the watch from functioning. There are no "water-free" watches, only waterproof ones. Likewise, Christianity does not promise a storm-free life. However, if we build our lives on biblical foundations, the storms of life will not destroy us. We cannot have lives that are storm-free, but we can become storm-proof.

We cannot have lives that
are storm-free, but we can
become storm-proof.

At Victory we have experienced quite a few storms as a church and as individuals. Some storms are simply the result of living in a fallen world. Other storms come in the form of persecution. In our churches around the world, people have been arrested, beaten, rejected by family, and fired from jobs. Some have laid their lives on the line for the sake of the gospel. Some live with death threats every day. In times of persecution, most have stood strong, but some have fallen away from the faith. Whether people stand or fall as believers depends more on the foundation than on the nature or intensity of the storm.

We know that all types of storms will eventually come our

way. We also know that every new follower of Jesus will experience storms. As disciples who are making disciples, our job is to help people dig deep, establish solid spiritual foundations, and prepare themselves spiritually to ride out whatever storms come their way. With those who have fallen away and come back, there is no condemnation. However, we also know that we have to work even harder to deepen and strengthen their spiritual foundations.

There are different starting points.

In construction, the foundation depends not only on the size of the building but also on the type of soil in the construction area. A builder does not lay the same type of foundation for a beach home and a mountain chalet. It is the same way when we establish spiritual foundations. Some elements are the same no matter where we are building, but other elements are added or deleted depending on the situation.

There are numerous lists outlining what should be included in new believer foundations. Rarely are two lists identical. Some consider the foundations listed in Hebrews 6 to be the foundations for all people for all time. I am not so sure about that. The Hebrews 6 list is the perfect starting point for *Hebrew* believers two thousand years ago. It fit perfectly into their worldview and their traditional Jewish theology. They already understood all six concepts in the list. However, this might not be the best starting point for Hindus who have a completely different view of sin, faith, resurrection, and eternity. While all the Hebrews 6 foundations are vital, they are not the only acceptable starting point for foundation laying. What you consider to be foundational depends on where new believers are coming from and the cultural baggage they bring along.

For example, in the Philippines, praying for new believers to receive the baptism in the Holy Spirit is easy. Coming from a very spiritual culture, new Filipino Christians typically experience the presence and power of the Holy Spirit with no hesitation. However, when it comes to water baptism, there are huge cultural, religious, and family obstacles to overcome. In other cultures, the relative ease and difficulty of establishing the spiritual foundations are completely reversed.

Generally speaking, if your church is reaching people from a culture where they have been surrounded by Christian ideas and influence, you will have a corresponding list of foundational concepts to convey. On the other extreme, if new believers have spent their lives as atheists, Jihadists, or tree worshipers, obviously foundations will begin at a different place. Just as we have to figure out the most effective way to engage our community for Christ, we also have to figure out the most effective way to establish spiritual foundations in each unique context.

Foundations are established by obedience to God's Word.

The passage in Luke 6 about houses with or without foundations is used all the time to emphasize the importance of teaching and learning fundamental elements of authentic Christianity—the doctrinal underpinnings of our faith such as incarnation, justification by faith, atonement, the nature and character of God, and so on. I recognize the importance of these biblical concepts and what can happen if disciples are not clear about what they believe. I also understand that there is a difference between knowing the truth about Jesus, believing the truth about Jesus, and actually following Jesus. You can know and believe all the right stuff but still not be His disciple.

That was precisely the point of Jesus's illustration. The two houses in the storm represented two kinds of people, both hearers of Jesus's words. How much teaching and learning a person received did not determine whether or not his spiritual foundations were considered deeply dug and founded on a rock. It was not catechisms, confessions of faith, or church membership. It was not his understanding the boundaries of orthodoxy. These things are certainly very important, and we work hard to help people learn them. However, in this illustration, a strong, enduring foundation was the result of *putting the Lord's words into practice*, not simply knowing the Word.

If we want to help believers develop a strong foundation, the thrust of our impartation should be focused on enabling them to practice Jesus's words, not just to understand or confess them. If we want to prepare young believers to withstand the storms of life, then we must teach them to consistently act on the Lord's command and to personally experience His promises.

Strong foundations that withstand the storms are constructed not only with the doctrine of the Word but also with the disciplines of following Christ and His Word. For example, it is not enough to merely teach about the preeminence of Christ; we must also challenge young believers to practice repentance and live a life of daily submission to His Lordship in all areas of life. It is not enough to simply teach the doctrine of the Holy Spirit; we must effectively lay our hands on them and pray for them to be baptized in the Spirit.

It is not enough to teach about the authority of Scripture and the power of prayer; we must help them cultivate the habit of daily prayer and Bible reading. It is not enough to teach them that God so loves the world; we must also equip and empower them to go and make disciples. The Great Commission in Matthew 28:18–20 mandates that we make disciples of all the nations. The last part of the passage explains *how* we are to make disciples: "teaching them to obey everything I have commanded you" (v. 20). Not just teaching, but teaching them to *obey*.

WHICH FOUNDATIONS?

As I have said before, making disciples is not primarily about helping church members become better church members. The commission to go and make disciples begins with engaging nonbelievers with the goal of sharing the gospel. However, it doesn't stop when people hear the gospel and receive Christ as their Lord and Savior. That is just the beginning. Now we need to establish biblical foundations, but where do we start? Consider what Paul wrote about his ministry of establishing foundations:

> By the grace God has given me, *I laid a foundation* as an expert builder, and someone else is building on it. But each one should be careful how he builds. *For no one can lay any foundation other than the one already laid, which is Jesus Christ.* If any man builds

on this foundation using gold, silver, costly stones, wood, hay or straw, his work will be shown for what it is, because the Day will bring it to light. It will be revealed with fire, and the fire will test the quality of each man's work. If what he has built survives, he will receive his reward. If it is burned up, he will suffer loss; he himself will be saved, but only as one escaping through the flames.

—1 Corinthians 3:10–15,
EMPHASIS ADDED

We can learn three basic lessons about foundations from these verses. First, there is really only one biblical foundation we can build our lives on, and that is the Lord Jesus Christ. Too often we build on the faulty foundations of religious tradition, personal experiences, church affiliation, or religious fads. Next, we find that it is possible to build on the *right* foundation with the *wrong* material. The right material is costly. Wrong material is cheap, temporary, and easily destroyed by fire. And finally, we see that God will test the quality of each person's work. Note that quantity and sincerity do not make up for lack of quality and obedience.

There is really only one biblical foundation we can build our lives on, and that is the Lord Jesus Christ.

After we have established Jesus as the ultimate foundation, what is next? When I talk about biblical foundations, from a practical perspective I am talking about establishing a believer in the *faith*, in the *Word*, and in the *church community*. Without these three essentials, few will be able to face life's storms without major destruction. These fundamentals are like a three-legged table; remove just one of these three foundations, and the table will topple.

Established in the faith

The starting point is being firmly established in "the faith that was once for all entrusted to the saints" (Jude 3). If a person is not established in the faith, he or she simply will not have a strong foundation or a storm-proof life. In Acts 2, when the Holy Spirit was poured out on the new church on the Day of Pentecost, Peter stood up and immediately started establishing the people in the faith. First, he preached Christ crucified, proclaiming Him as "both Lord and Messiah" (Acts 2:36, NLT). Then he said the proper response would be to "repent and be baptized, everyone of you" (v. 38). He went on to talk about receiving the gift of the Holy Spirit and being added to the fellowship.

So when I talk about a new believer being established in the faith, I am talking about faith in Christ, repentance, baptism, and being filled with the Holy Spirit. That's the basic starting point.

Established in the Word

After a person is established in the faith, the next step is to start a personal habit of daily Bible reading. No one can survive the storms of life without the power of God's Word. Jesus told His original disciples that they were truly His disciples if they held to His Word. The apostle Peter explained the importance of the Word this way: "Like newborn babies, long for the pure milk of the word, so that by it you may grow in respect to salvation" (1 Pet. 2:2, NAS). Just as a newborn baby needs milk to grow, newborn disciples need the milk of God's Word.

I am thankful that when I was a new believer, Ron Musselman, my youth leader, strongly emphasized daily devotional Bible reading, personal Bible study, Bible memorization, weekly small group Bible study, and, most of all, Bible obedience. He made it his top priority to establish me in the Word. Ron knew that if he did not help me develop the habit of Bible reading, I would lean and crash when the storms hit.

I remember the first time I attended Ron's little discipleship group. I was a brand-new believer with a brand-new Living Bible, the one with a green padded cover. At the end of that meeting Ron announced that our homework was Psalm chapter 1. I thought, "One chapter, Book of Psalms, shouldn't be too hard to find." That seemed doable. Then I found out that he intended for us to memorize it.

Memorize it! I was pretty lazy when it came to reading or studying anything. In our house, baseball batting averages, football yards per carry, and basketball free throw percentages were more important than grade point averages. So there was not a lot of pressure when it came to homework. I never wasted time watching television or movies because I was too busy hunting, fishing, or playing sports. But neither had I ever, in my entire short life, read a whole book. I sometimes skimmed through CliffsNotes summaries, but I never read the book.

It is a good thing my wife, Deborah, came from a very different background and perspective regarding academics. When our sons were smaller, she didn't like me talking to them about their academic career. I was likely to say, "Sure you can play basketball after school. Don't worry about that homework. You can finish it tomorrow on the bus or during lunch period."

After becoming a Christian, I eventually turned into a voracious reader. At the beginning, however, I really needed some accountability. Simply reading Psalm 1 would have been a giant leap forward for me. At the next meeting I stumbled through a recitation that was in a few places remotely similar to Psalm 1. What I considered to be my all-time best effort at Bible memorization did not measure up to Ron's standard. "I said to memorize," was his only response.

For the next eighteen months Ron Musselman held me accountable to read, study, memorize, and live God's Word. I knew every time I saw him that he would ask two questions: had I been reading my Bible every day since the last time I saw him, and how were my parents doing. If I saw Ron today, thirty-three years after I graduated from high school, he would probably ask me if I had been reading my Bible every day since the last time he saw me.

I did eventually memorize Psalm 1 and still remember it today.

> Blessed is the man who does not walk in the counsel
> of the wicked or stand in the way of sinners or sit
> in the seat of mockers. But his delight is in the law
> of the LORD, and on his law he meditates day and
> night. He is like a tree planted by streams of water,
> which yields its fruit in season and whose leaf does
> not wither. Whatever he does prospers.
>
> —PSALM 1:1–3

That passage was not an arbitrary selection. Ron chose it to lay the groundwork for a spiritual foundation in my life. Those verses paint a picture of a new believer who had developed the discipline of reading and meditating on God's Word every day and night. The roots of God's Word were planted so deeply that they remained strong in very dry times. Deep roots are synonymous with a rock-solid, storm-proof spiritual foundation.

There are many helpful tools for Bible reading and Bible study. Rice Broocks and I wrote *The Purple Book* for the same reason—to help establish believers in the Word. *The Purple Book* is basically a guided tour through different parts of the Bible, from Genesis to Revelation, touching on a dozen foundational topics.

Established in the church community

When Jesus called His first disciples to follow Him, they had to follow along with other disciples. They did not have the option of following alone. They were added to the group, to His small community of cross-carrying disciples. Being a disciple is and always has been a team sport, a group activity, a family affair, a community event. It is not a solo flight or an individual achievement. On the Day of Pentecost, after Peter preached Christ crucified, called the people to repentance, baptized them, and ministered the Holy Spirit, it was not over. That was still the beginning. "Those who accepted his message were baptized, and about three thousand *were added to their number* that day" (Acts 2:41, emphasis added). Then the Bible describes the believers as being "devoted...to the fellowship" (v. 42) and being together and united in community. In that context, "the Lord added to their number daily those who were being saved" (v. 47). Living in community with other believers helps storm-proof our lives.

CONSEQUENCES OF INADEQUATE FOUNDATIONS

The main building on the campus of Philippine Christian College (PCC) in Cabanatuan City was built in 1964 with three stories. Several years later three additional floors were added, making it the tallest building in Cabanatuan. All seemed well until a 7.8 magnitude earthquake struck at 4:26 p.m. on July 16, 1990.[7]

I'll never forget that moment. I was at home in Manila talking on the phone with my friend Julius Fabregas, when suddenly my floor started vibrating and my bookshelves shook. Julius dropped his phone mid-sentence and ran to see if his daughter was OK. She was. I walked outside expecting to see crumbling buildings. Fortunately, there was little damage in Manila. But 170 kilometers away in Cabanatuan, it was a different story.

The six-story PCC building collapsed, crushing 154 students and faculty to death, and injuring another hundred. It was the only building in the city to fall.[8] The foundations held up for years, even with the additional three floors, until the shaking started. The earthquake proved that the foundations were inadequate for six floors. Tragedy ensued, not only because of the strength of the earthquake but also because of faulty foundations.

WikiChurch Lessons

WikiChurches are built on strong biblical foundations. Too many Christians are leaning and falling, not because of the intensity of the storms, but because of weak foundations. Storms in the Christian life are inevitable, but we can storm-proof our lives and the lives of the people we disciple by *establishing biblical foundations*. It is not enough to have a good façade; we must build strong foundations by establishing believers in the faith, in the Word, and in the church community. Once the foundations are in place, it is time to be *equipped*.

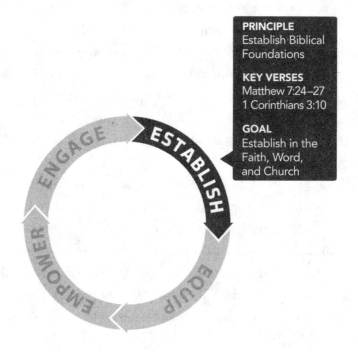

PRINCIPLE
Establish Biblical
Foundations

KEY VERSES
Matthew 7:24–27
1 Corinthians 3:10

GOAL
Establish in the
Faith, Word,
and Church

CHAPTER SEVEN

THE MYTH
OF MATURITY

ECAUSE OUR CHURCH constantly plants new churches
and new congregations, it seems as if we are always
in the process of equipping new worship leaders. Joey
was a talented singer and musician, but his first few times in
the spotlight were rough. After a staff meeting (that didn't
include Joey), the head of the worship department suggested
that he switch worship leaders the following week because
we had a big-shot foreign guest preacher scheduled. When I
asked why, he mentioned our guest speaker and reminded me
that the last time Joey led worship, it was forgettable. I said
that I was well aware we were hosting the big-shot American
and that Joey wasn't our best. However, I did not see any

reason to bump Joey from the schedule. The discussion ended with me reminding our entire staff that we weren't trying to impress our guest speaker—in fact, he had better impress us or he wouldn't be invited back.

For me, it's more important to equip a worship leader than to have a perfect worship service. I knew that if we rescheduled Joey, it would shatter his confidence and set the equipping process back a few months. When Sunday came around, Joey led worship and our guest preached. Sure, the worship was less than average, but Joey went on to become a good worship leader and a great pastor.

We hear the phrase all the time: "Every member a minister." Yet because of our performance-driven culture, we often have little tolerance for the messiness of the equipping process. We do church as if only professional ministers should do ministry. The biblical job description for professional ministers—apostles, prophets, evangelists, pastors, and teachers—is to equip the "non-pros" for ministry, then get out of their way. When we forget that, we forget one of the primary reasons God called us to serve in the first place.

BUSTING
DISCIPLESHIP MYTHS

Have you ever watched the *MythBusters* show on Discovery Channel? I watched it once, and it changed my life. Not my whole life, just the rainy days. Because of *MythBusters*, I no longer feel compelled to run when it rains. Now I walk. And I'm dry. Not totally, but dry enough. Somehow those mad scientists with the unruly facial hair proved that running in the rain makes one wetter than walking in the rain. Hard to believe, but it's true. This is valuable information, especially for men, since real men don't carry umbrellas.

A myth is a commonly held belief that is not true. We believe myths because other people believe them or because a person in a position of authority told us the myth was true. For instance, as children most of us believed that gifts appeared in our homes on December 25 because a fat white dude with a homeless man beard, a red suit, and flying reindeers squeezed down our chimneys, left gifts, then flew back to the North Pole to hang out with pointy-eared short people. We believed this even if our home did not have a fireplace because of the credibility of the person who told us and because all our friends seemed to believe the same thing.

---

*It's time to outgrow and bust
some discipleship myths.*

Eventually we got smart and outgrew the Santa myth and hopefully other myths. I think it's time to outgrow and bust some discipleship myths that have been passed down from generation to generation. Here are three popular discipleship myths—propagated by thousands of well-meaning pastors and professional religious leaders—that have paralyzed and imprisoned millions of believers all over the world.

1. The Myth of Mentoring—*My pastor's job is to minister to me.* This myth causes church people

to demand that pastors spoon-feed them, care for them, and meet all their spiritual needs. It turns pastors into spiritual pseudo-superheroes and regular Christians into passive spectators at religious shows.

2. The Myth of Ministry—*I am not yet ready to be used by God.* This myth convinces people they don't pray enough, aren't mature enough, don't know enough Bible verses, have too many past sins, are too young, and so on to keep them from engaging in ministry. I'm sure you can add a few more spiritual excuses to this list.

3. The Myth of Maturity—*No one should minister until he is mature.* This myth convinces believers that before they even attempt to minister to others, they need another discipleship class, training course, leadership seminar, and framed certificate on their wall. Only then would they possibly be mature enough to be used by God.

As spiritual as they may sound, these three statements are false. They are commonly held beliefs that are not true, yet we hear them over and over. Let's look at God's Word and see if we can bust these myths.

The apostle Paul had a meteoric rise from church persecutor to church leader. First he was "breathing out murderous threats against the Lord's disciples" (Acts 9:1), tossing men and women into prison simply because they were followers of Christ. While on his way to Damascus to persecute more believers, he had a close encounter with the risen Lord, resulting in a 180-degree turn. An ordinary disciple—not an apostle, prophet, or pastor—named Ananias established biblical foundations in Paul's life.

Then Paul spent "several days" (v. 19) with the disciples, and "at once" (v. 20) he began to preach and make disciples. Then "after many days" (v. 23)—not years, months, or weeks, but *days*—Paul's preaching stirred up persecution, and he had to flee for his life. Then an older disciple named Barnabas believed in Paul and took him under his wing when others were not so sure Paul was ready to be used by God.

Paul did not wait until he was mature to start ministering. Rather, he matured rapidly because he ministered and because he had other disciples such as Ananias and Barnabas as mentors.

LEARNING
HOW TO COUNT

This same Paul, who started ministering to others as soon as he had his life-changing encounter with Jesus, wrote about the secret of spiritual maturity in his letter to the Ephesians.

> It was he [Jesus] who gave some to be apostles, some to be prophets, some to be evangelists, and some to be pastors and teachers, to prepare God's people for works of service, so that the body of Christ may be built up until we all reach unity in the faith and in the knowledge of the Son of God

> and become mature, attaining to the whole measure
> of the fullness of Christ.
>
> —Ephesians 4:11–13

In verse 11 Paul identified the mentors as apostles, prophets, evangelists, pastors, and teachers. In verse 12 he gave their job description: "to prepare God's people for works of service." The New King James version translates that job description as "equipping…the saints for the work of ministry." The practical application of this passage at Victory is that the professional, full-time pastors, teachers, and church staff believe their primary role is to serve as mentors. Their task is to *equip* every believer for the work of the ministry. It is not to do all the ministry, but to *equip* all the people to do it. Their top priority is to equip disciples to do ministry and to make disciples.

Do you spend more time ministering to
people or preparing people to minister?

I made this point once when I was speaking at a leadership conference in Singapore to about 120 of our Asian pastors, missionaries, and church planters. Some were from China; others were pioneering churches in Iran, Mongolia, Vietnam, and Bangladesh. Many had experienced intense persecution. Others were expecting it soon. There was not an ounce of laziness or apathy in that room. I knew that these young men and women were all aggressive, hardworking, high-commitment people who were willing and ready to do anything for the sake of the gospel. My opening comment to them was, "If you're not experiencing the kind of fruitfulness you desire, it's not because you are too lazy to minister. Quite the contrary, it might be because you minister too much."

I went on to say that ministering too much will prevent many church planters from getting to the next level of growth or will prevent disciple-makers from seeing their small groups grow and multiply.

Next, I posed a question to them, the same query I constantly ask the leaders I work with: "Do you spend more time ministering to people or preparing people to minister? Do you spend more time preparing messages or preparing people?"

No matter what your church responsibilities are, you can prepare others for the same ministry. If you are a worship leader, are you preparing others to be worship leaders? If you are a campus missionary, are you equipping others to be campus missionaries? For that idea to work its way through the entire organization, it has to be the prevailing culture from top to bottom. It does not work if the senior leader is the primary minister rather than the primary equipper.

Most of the world counts like this: eleven, twelve, then thirteen. In Ephesians 4, verse 11 identifies the *mentors*. Verse 12 introduces the *ministers*. Then, according to verse 13, we become *mature*. Too many church leaders, however, do not follow that order. For them it is more like eleven, thirteen, then twelve. They count differently because they think differently—the *mentors*, or professional religious workers, do most of the ministry (that's verse 11), then *maturity* happens because of the mentors (verse 13), and finally *ministry* happens (verse 12) only after a person reaches a mysterious undefined nirvana state of spiritual maturity. Often that is on a provisional basis until they complete their religious degree and hang a diploma on their wall.

Unfortunately, that means spending years studying ideas that few care about and only the initiated understand. After the fledgling leader has learned the new religious language and forgotten how to communicate with and engage non-believers, after he has been completely baptized into the Christian community and has lost touch with the nuances of his culture and community, and after he no longer has any non-Christian friends, he is now ready to be certified as an official minister. Fortunately there is a better way, a more biblical way. All we have to do is remember how to count: eleven, twelve, thirteen—not eleven, thirteen, twelve!

In the New Testament times, ministry was the pathway to maturity—eleven, twelve, then thirteen. Today, knowledge has replaced ministry as the pathway to maturity. This new way may not produce spiritually mature leaders, but at least we have religious leaders with advanced degrees, nice personal libraries, and impressive vocabularies. We've also done a good job of replacing lifestyle discipleship with classes, programs, and manuals.

THREE
DISCIPLESHIP TRUTHS

A few paragraphs ago I mentioned three common discipleship myths. Here are three disciple truths based on Ephesians 4 that, I hope, will bust those destructive myths forever.

1. The Truth of Mentoring: A pastor's job is not primarily to minister to people but to equip people to minister to *others*. Life, church, and ministry are not about the people in the pews. They are about God and others (Eph. 4:11).

2. The Truth of Ministry: While some members may not feel ready *yet*, God is ready to use them *now*—even if they think they don't pray enough, aren't mature enough, don't know enough Bible verses, or have too many past sins. Even if they're too young or lost their temper yesterday and used a word the pastor would never use on Sunday, God wants to use them (Eph. 4:12).

3. The Truth of Maturity: We can't wait until every believer *feels* mature enough to minister because no one will mature *unless* they minister. This is one of those chicken and egg conundrums. Which comes first—ministry or maturity? According to the Bible, ministry comes first. Remember eleven, twelve, then thirteen—not eleven, thirteen, then twelve (Eph. 4:13).

Is It Possible to Minister Too Much?

Now that we have busted the myth of maturity and established that ministry is the biblical pathway to maturity, let's look at the equipping process. Several years ago Rice Broocks and I were in Hawaii talking to a group of pastors and church leaders who wanted to join our ministry, Every Nation Churches. Rice was trying to explain the nuts and bolts of our in-house, church-based ministry training school, Every Nation Leadership Institute (ENLI). In front of the group, Rice turned to me and asked, "Steve, would you say that ENLI is the key to all the great leaders who have been raised up in Victory–Philippines?"

Without hesitating, I simply said, "No."

That was not the answer Rice was expecting. Thinking that I had misunderstood what he was trying to do, he rephrased the question and pitched it to me again. Again my answer to his question about ENLI being the key to developing strong leaders in the Philippines was simply, "No."

Rice kept trying to get a yes out of me, but it kept coming out no. Everyone began to chuckle at the obvious fact that the two guys up front were not reading off the same script. Finally Rice said, "OK, Steve, explain what you mean."

"The key is discipleship," I said. "If we think that a once-a-week, three-hour Bible study in a classroom is going to make disciples, equip ministers, and develop leaders, we are mistaken. Classrooms and training courses like ENLI are important supplements to the discipleship process—but they are the supplement, not the core." Of course, Rice agreed.

Jesus ministered to large groups of people. He fed them, taught them, and healed them. But His prime time was invested in small group discipleship. Jesus continually challenged His disciples to put their faith into practice by sending them out to *do* great things, not just to *learn* great things and to teach great things.

In the previous chapter we talked about the parable of the two houses—one with a foundation dug deep and established on the rock, and the other with no foundation at all. You know what happened to each house when the storm came. The fragile house represented those who merely heard the words of Jesus. In other words, they had attended His big meetings and were familiar with His teachings. The storm-proof house represented those who heard the words of Jesus but who had also learned how to put them into practice. They were discipled and became mature as they engaged in ministry.

The biblical pattern is that mentors equip, then the people minister, resulting in maturity—eleven, twelve, then thirteen. If you really want to grow up in God, you find your mentors and start ministering. The myth of maturity is that people should not minister to others until they have reached maturity.

The Victory *equipping and empowering* principles are based on a conviction that all disciples should make disciples. Sadly, many who have been in church a long time accept the myth of maturity and refuse to minister. They naïvely postpone ministry until they mature, but unfortunately they are hoping for a maturity that will never come from the passing of time, the acquisition of knowledge, or attendance in a discipleship course. As difficult as it is to change, it is time to reject the myth and start ministering, whether you feel ready or not.

Even the group of Asian pastors in Singapore who had not grown up in Western churches had a hard time processing these two concepts:

1. If your church is not growing, then perhaps you (as the mentor) are spending too much time ministering to people and not enough time equipping people to minister.

2. If your people are not maturing very quickly, then perhaps you are taking too long to get them equipped and empowered to do the work of the ministry. The more they minister today, the more they will mature tomorrow.

WHERE DID ALL THESE LEADERS COME FROM?

When pastors and Christian leaders visit Victory–Manila, what they frequently comment on is not the size of our church. That is partly because they cannot see the church as a whole on a single visit. They would have to attend about eighty-one weekend worship services in fifteen venues to get a sense of our size. I am the founding pastor, and I have not visited all of the congregations. What they do comment on with great regularity is the number of young leaders at Victory who, to them, seem spiritually mature beyond their age. We are often asked, "Where do you get all these leaders?"

If you spent some time at Victory–Manila, you would see that we have some really good training programs such as Victory Weekend, which is followed by our ten-week "Training for Victory" course. The training materials Victory produces are simply guides to help people study the Bible without a lot of commentary. If you read through the curriculum, you would see that it consists of pretty straightforward study material on basic Christian living topics—nothing unique or special. We also have some young preachers who are doing a great job.

The training materials, the classes, and the preaching are good but not so remarkable that they can account for our constant stream of young leaders. Perhaps that is why the phenomena of emerging leadership is so bewildering to those who are trying to discover its source. Whatever success we have had equipping and empowering next-generation leaders at Victory is not the result of our preaching, our programs, or our publishing. It is the inevitable result of our discipleship culture and our relentless commitment to a simple discipleship process.

There is not some secret ingredient that, if applied to a local church context, will automatically produce consistent growth in size and maturity. Church growth, spiritual health, and moral strength are always the result of several things working together. Yet there is a principle we adopted many years ago that, as much or more than any other idea, has been responsible for year after year of consistent growth in the number of disciples and the rapid emergence of next-generation Filipino leadership. It is the central underlying idea that *every* disciple should make disciples—not many, not most, but *every* disciple should make disciples. Not just church staff, not just "mature" Christians, and not just evangelistic types. Regardless of travel and work schedules, status, gender, or age, *every disciple should make disciples.*

What about young people? Should they make disciples? They do at Victory. Before and after all our worship services and youth meetings, we have dozens of student-led discipleship groups gathering in different parts of the building, on the front steps, or throughout the mall (nine of our congregations meet in Manila malls). These teens are not waiting for a professional youth pastor or campus minister to make disciples. They have been equipped and empowered to make disciples, knowing that the more they minister to others, the more they mature.

Do we really believe new believers are qualified to disciple others? Of course we do. A disciple is a person who follows Jesus. Discipleship is the process of helping someone follow Jesus. As long as someone is following Jesus, that person should be helping others follow Him. We are not talking about teaching Old Testament survey or systematic theology. We encourage new believers who are learning about faith, repentance, forgiveness, and prayer to teach their friends what they are learning.

What about disciples who still have some character issues? If you think a person's lack of character disqualifies him or her from making disciples, what about your own lack? Typically the character flaws people point out as proof that someone is not qualified to make disciples are the issues with which those doing the complaining have no problem. Most of us judge other people's issues harshly and our own with much grace. If God's spotlight were to shine on each of us, who would not have some character problems revealed? I have been asked many times, "How do you know when someone is ready to start discipling others?" My response is usually this: "If they have repented, crossed the line of faith, accepted Christ, and are not rebelliously continuing in some major blatant sin, then they're ready."

Often the biggest issue young believers have to overcome is their own lack of confidence about being ready to minister to their friends. What they really need are leaders who encourage, equip, and empower them to make disciples, not critics who think they are helping the Holy Spirit by pointing out character issues.

The last thing anyone needs is some older Christian confirming their doubts and fears and making sure zealous young Christians "stay in their place." It usually does not take much to discourage young believers from making disciples.

JUST STAY ONE CHAPTER AHEAD

Whatever process your church or organization adopts, it has to grow out of your core beliefs. The Victory process of *equipping* and *empowering* young disciples to minister has developed into its current form simply because we believe that anybody making any progress with God should be making disciples—anyone following Jesus should help others follow Him. If we did not believe this, our process would be very, very different.

When we started in the Philippines, Rice was the main speaker in the big meetings. As I noted in the early chapters, I was woefully ineffective as an evangelistic speaker. I still am. My job was to minister to those people who responded to Rice's message and help them understand grace, faith, and repentance. Then I taught them about the Holy Spirit and prepared them to be baptized in water. The next week I would begin training them to do the same thing with the next wave of Filipino students who would come to Christ in the following days.

I can remember saying to Ferdie Cabiling, "I'm going to train you to do this because we are all going back to the United States in a few weeks."

Just stay one chapter ahead.

Ferdie replied, "But I've only been saved three days!"

"Yes, but this guy has only been saved three minutes, and to him you're a spiritual giant. Remember I told you to read the Book of Mark? How far have you read?"

Ferdie eagerly replied, "I've already finished Mark, and I'm almost finished with Luke."

Then I told him what has become a constantly repeated Victory slogan, *"Just stay one chapter ahead.* As long as you stay one chapter ahead, you can disciple him, but if he passes you, then he will disciple you."

That is how we built the church at the very beginning. Because we were leaving, we accepted the idea (out of necessity) that every disciple should be equipped and empowered to make disciples. What we have come to understand is that being disciples and making disciples is just as much a necessity for Victory now as it was at the beginning. Sure, we now have hundreds of seasoned ministers whom we could deploy to meet any ministerial need. However, we cannot make more disciples, nor can we make them more mature, if we abandon that original idea.

Every disciple should make disciples. In an earlier chapter I referred to once being asked why so many young believers at Victory seem to display such maturity. It was my wife, Deborah, who zeroed in on the key issue. "Everything we did," she said, "was with the idea of leaving. We weren't building a ministry for ourselves. We were preparing eighteen- to twenty-year-old Filipinos to do the ministry and lead the church."

The apostle Paul wrote to one of his young ministers, "The reason I left you in Crete was that you might straighten out what was left unfinished and appoint elders in every town, as I directed you" (Titus 1:5). The mission, as Paul and his team understood it, was to establish, equip, empower, and get out of town.

A DISCIPLESHIP
REFORMATION

In the early days, we were preparing to physically leave the country. However, when the team went on to South Korea, we were *left behind* (but that is another book—a work of fiction I believe, written by someone else who borrowed my title). After we all returned to the United States, God called Deborah and me to return. Now it has been twenty-seven years, and through all those years we still tried to maintain that leaving mentality. I am always in training mode, always looking to equip and empower someone to do whatever I am doing. I insist that all leadership team members have that same mentality. Even if we are not physically leaving the country, we are urgently equipping new believers because it is our full intention to "leave them" in charge of ministering to others.

Sometimes with all the efforts to "learn one's way into success," people actually learn their way out of it. In other words, they quickly move on from the simple ideas that God uses in order to discover more sophisticated concepts that require years of training to understand. The result is that ministry and discipleship become far too complex for most believers and turn into the exclusive domain of elite, professional Christians. That was one of the problems of the scribes and Pharisees. Being one of their disciples was so complex and time-consuming that no one could do it unless they worked at it on a full-time basis.

There are a lot of similarities between the traditions of the Pharisees and the church at the beginning of the sixteenth century. One of the ideas that drove the Protestant Reformation was the priesthood of all believers. The reformers asserted that it was not just a few specially gifted, specially trained, specially called people who had access to God. Every believer of every age, gender, economic status, and academic degree had the ability come to the Father through Jesus Christ, our mediator and our high priest.

At Victory we have adopted what might be called a "discipleship reformation," where all believers are equipped and empowered to minister, not just a few professionals with advanced training and a decade of experience. This is a revolutionary idea but not a new one. I had heard and believed this for years. However, I was never really serious enough about what I said I believed to act on it. I suppose that is the difference between intellectual belief and true faith. When the Victory team did begin to act as if we really believed all disciples should make disciples, it took our church to a new level. Discipleship had always been a big deal at Victory. The problem is that few, besides the pastors and campus missionaries, were actually attempting to make disciples. But when making disciples became the ministry of *every disciple*, not just the leaders, we were no longer simply adding disciples—we started multiplying.

FULL-TIME IS NOT A CALLING

Several years ago a student scheduled an urgent appointment with me. As soon as he walked in my office, before he even sat down, he blurted out, "Pastor, I want to go full-time."

I had no idea what he wanted when he set the appointment, but I certainly was not expecting this. "Full-time what?" I asked.

"Umm, I don't know, just full-time ministry, maybe—like you, Jun, and Ferdie."

He was new in church and probably had no clue what Jun, Ferdie, or I actually did on a daily basis. "So you want to minister?" I asked. I was trying to get him focused on the concept of ministering to people rather than ministry as a position or an occupation. He didn't respond, just looked at me. I asked, "What exactly do you want to do in ministry?"

"Umm, I don't know. I guess I am open to any kind of full-time position."

"Anything but finishing college," I thought to myself.

"How long until you graduate?" I asked him.

"I don't want to waste any more time going to college. I feel called to go full-time now."

As the conversation went on, I discovered he was struggling in a couple of classes, thus the urgency to be a full-time minister. I tried to explain to my friend that full-time was not a calling. Whether you are a student, a teacher, a factory worker, or the factory owner, every Christian is to represent Christ full-time, no matter the source of his or her paycheck. I am not sure if my subtle corrections had much of an impact on my zealous young friend. He left with most of the same ideas with which he had arrived. He assumed that if one loves God wholeheartedly, anything short of full-time ministry would be some sort of compromise.

The fact that we have a lot of young leaders at Victory causes some to conclude that we regularly challenge our people to go into the ministry or that we hold up the idea of full-time ministry as the "high calling." Actually, it is almost completely the opposite. We do everything we can to equip and empower every person to minister. However, ministering to people and becoming a professional church employee are two very different things. I have had numerous conversations with people who were very effective witnesses for Christ as teachers, business owners, or professionals. Because they were successful in ministry, they assumed the next step was to quit their jobs to become full-time church professionals.

"Why would you want to do that?" is my usual reply. In

most cases the ability to effectively engage people for Christ is the result of their careers or places of employment. When someone becomes a professional minister, he or she loses a great deal of commonality and connectivity with nonchurch people. My conversations with aspiring full-time ministers eventually get down to the basic question: "What do you feel called to do—minister to people, 'be in the ministry,' or both?"

There is, of course, no automatic answer here. There have been many instances in which people were so effectively engaging their culture and community and establishing biblical foundations that they simply no longer had time to continue their day jobs. Whether or not they continued working a secular job had no effect on their ability to make disciples. However, there have been many others whose effectiveness is undoubtedly connected to the strategic place God has put them.

The idea of going into full-time ministry because you desire to minister to people makes perfect sense if you are used to thinking like traditional Western church leaders— in other words, if you think the primary ones who do ministry are mentors (apostles, prophets, evangelists, pastors, and teachers). However, going into full-time ministry to minister makes little sense if you understand that the primary role of professional ministers is to equip and empower the people in the church to do the work of the ministry. Going into full-time ministry is like taking the best fighter pilot in the air force out of the cockpit and reassigning him or her to the training school. That would be a great move if the pilot's desire were to be a trainer. But if his greatest desire is to be on the front lines engaging the enemy as a fighter pilot, it makes little sense. The same question arises, "Why would you want to do that?"

Church Is a
Volunteer Organization

Several years ago I was invited to Australia to teach on discipleship—our one and only spiritual judo move. Mark was my host. He leads a dynamic church of more than five thousand people in Queensland. Mark is in his fifties, but his church is filled with young people. His music team and his worship services are the best. I was there to teach discipleship, but I also learned a lot by observing Mark's leadership.

Mark and his team seemed particularly shocked by and interested in our paid staff to membership ratio. At the time about twenty-nine thousand people were attending Victory–Manila, with about seven thousand of them at our Fort Bonifacio location. What impressed Mark was the number *nineteen*. Victory–Fort Bonifacio had seven thousand people and only nineteen paid staff. All fifteen Victory–Manila congregations have roughly the same paid staff ratio as the Fort congregation.

---

*The church is basically a
volunteer organization.*

Mark's church had fewer people and more than three times the number of paid staff. He wanted to know why. What was the secret? Simple: we equip all believers to do ministry, then we empower them to make disciples. Because we have thousands of trained *ministers*, we do not need a huge staff. Mark decided to visit Victory–Manila to see for himself. I was out of the country, so he shadowed Joey, Paolo, Robert, and other Victory leaders. Mark saw both a *discipleship culture* and a simple *discipleship process* that empowers thousands of ordinary people to effectively minister to their friends and relatives.

We believe that the church is basically a volunteer organization. There are, of course, functions that full-time paid staff have to carry out. Nonetheless, the more we operate as a volunteer organization, the healthier and more effective the church becomes. An added benefit is that we are able to invest millions of pesos into cross-cultural missions, church planting, and ministry to the poor. Our full-time paid staff understand they are the mentors who equip volunteers to do ministry. Consequently, most of the ministry work—evangelism, discipleship, hospital visitation, encouragement, community service—is conducted by volunteers, not by paid professionals.

WikiChurch Lessons

WikiChurches are intentional about *equipping*. At Victory, this process is pretty simple. Full-time leaders train believers to do basic Christian ministry—share the gospel, lead people to Christ, pray for them to be filled with the Holy Spirit. Rather than paying a small army of full-time ministers, average people do the work of the ministry. And because they are no longer spectators but ministers, they are on the fast track to maturity.

The church grows in size and maturity, the budget shrinks, and the process perpetuates itself. While the *equipping* process can be implemented in a single staff meeting, developing an equipping culture takes time. It all begins with a biblical mentality—a consistent way of thinking based on a clearly defined belief that all disciples should make disciples. And it helps if we know how to count—eleven, twelve, then thirteen.

And when believers are equipped to minister, it is then time to *empower*.

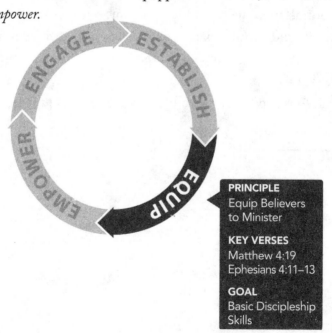

PRINCIPLE
Equip Believers
to Minister

KEY VERSES
Matthew 4:19
Ephesians 4:11–13

GOAL
Basic Discipleship
Skills

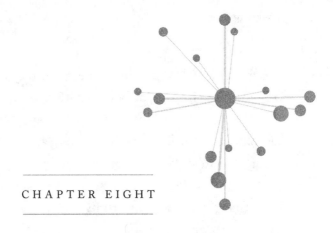

CHAPTER EIGHT

THE MAN OF
GOD SYNDROME

W HEN DEBORAH AND I landed in the Philippines in 1984, we were one of the most ill-equipped and unprepared missionaries to ever leave America. We had no mission training, no cross-cultural understanding, and almost no support. But, in our minds at the time, none of that mattered because we were *empowered*. Sure, a little equipping and some financial support would have made life easier, but at least we were off the bench and in the game.

In those days we were part of Maranatha Campus Ministries, a ministry that specialized in reaching university students and sending them to start campus churches that would reach the world. We didn't quite reach the whole world before the ministry imploded, but we sure gave it our best shot.

Being a ministry that mobilized youth, Maranatha people accomplished a lot in a hurry and at the same time made countless mistakes, as young people are prone to do. But, despite the youthful mistakes, I will always appreciate the fact that I got the opportunity to do something significant at a young age. I am grateful that I was empowered, that I did not have to wait until I was thirty before God might use me. No, in Maranatha we believed that God could use young people right now.

The Most Empowering Leader Ever

Jesus modeled an empowering leadership style. Of course, He was wise enough to equip them first and to continue ongoing evaluation and equipping after He empowered them. He taught, healed, and fed huge crowds, but equipping took place primarily in a small group setting. The small group is where He explained the meaning of the parables, revealed His purposes, and warned about things that would be an unavoidable part of their future. The small group is where Jesus dealt with personal issues and attitudes.

However, His small discipleship group was not an endless, inward-looking group therapy session. The whole point of small group discipleship was to equip and empower every disciple to make disciples. The goal was to send them out to replicate what He had been doing—to teach what He had been teaching and to minister to people as He had been ministering. Here is how Luke described it.

> When Jesus had called the Twelve together, he gave
> them power and authority to drive out all demons
> and to cure diseases, and he sent them out to preach
> the kingdom of God and to heal the sick.
>
> —Luke 9:1–2

After equipping, empowering, and sending them out, Jesus always had debriefing sessions when His disciples returned. They reported victories and defeats. They asked questions. Jesus corrected their lack of faith and their selfish attitudes. The equipping process did not end when they were empowered; it continued and intensified *after* they were empowered. The more they were empowered, the more they were equipped. And the more they were equipped, the more they were empowered. It was an ongoing cycle.

The whole point of small group discipleship is to equip and empower every disciple to make disciples.

Jesus was never *content* for disciples to simply follow Him as spectators but was *intent* on empowering them to do what He had been doing. He went so far as to say that they would do even greater works after He had gone back to the Father. It was one thing to follow Jesus, but standing in for Him as a minister was something else altogether. What thoughts must have run through the minds of the twelve when Jesus said, "OK, now I am sending you out to do what I have been doing."

"Are you kidding? I'm a fisherman," Andrew might have said.

"You cannot be serious," John could have added.

Perhaps Matthew, the former tax collector, objected, "Jesus, have You considered the fact that I am one of the most hated people in this nation?"

"Not sure we are quite ready for this," they all must have thought.

The disciples were, in fact, repeatedly astonished at what Jesus expected of them. When confronted with an impossible logistical situation, Jesus said, "Why don't you give the multitude something to eat?" (Matt. 14:15–16). When faced with a life-threatening storm in the middle of the Sea of Galilee, He asked them, "Where is your faith?" (Luke 8:24–25). When they found themselves confronted with demonic forces they could not cast out, Jesus said, "Oh, unbelieving generation. How long shall I be with you?" (Matt. 17:16–18).

It was as if Jesus was suggesting to the twelve that they had better figure out how to do those things quickly because He was not going to be with them much longer. He was "leading with the idea of leaving." Consequently, equipping and empowering them to minister and to make disciples became His highest priority.

In the previous chapter I talked about challenging a group of Asian leaders concerning whether or not they were ministering too much rather than equipping others to minister. I could have issued a similar challenge with regard to empowering. If we are not seeing next-generation disciples consistently emerging as leaders empowered to minister, then perhaps we need to begin to think about leaving. A "leaving mentality" could mean moving on to plant another church, getting out of town, or just getting out of the way.

SPIRITUALLY
TRANSMITTED DISEASES

I had an interesting conversation about a year ago. I had been out of the country—simultaneously getting things done and getting out of the way. On Friday afternoon I was walking out of my office in the Every Nation building in Fort Bonifacio when I saw a white guy standing in the parking lot. He seemed to be waiting for someone.

I extended my hand, "Hi! Howya doing? I'm Steve."

White Guy: "Nice to meet you, Steve. I'm new here. Moved to Manila two months ago."

Me: "Oh, where's home?"

White Guy: "Nashville."

Me and White Guy: Small talk about Nashville and White Guy's job.

White Guy: "You go to church here?"

Me: "Sometimes."

About this time a church member walked by and shouted, "Hey, Pastor Steve! Welcome back. Are you preaching this weekend?"

I waved at Church Member, smiled at White Guy, got in my car, and drove home. White Guy had been attending

Victory for about eight weeks. He had never seen me nor heard me preach. In fact, he had never heard of Steve Murrell. That is really not too uncommon because, you see, Victory in the Philippines is not about me. Never has been. Never will be.

One thing that haunts and hinders much of the church in the Western world is what I call the "Man of God syndrome," or MOGS for short. This highly contagious MOGS cripples empowerment by promoting a leadership paradigm in which the senior leader resembles Moses, Elijah, or even an Eastern holy man rather than the New Testament servant-leader. What follows that mistaken profile is the hope that if we could just get near to the great hero-preacher, then the anointing of God would somehow trickle down to us.

We don't have to look only in charismatic and Pentecostal circles to find the Man of God syndrome. Personality-driven leadership is an attitude, not a theology. You find it in corporations, Christian ministries, and most brands of church. It has become so deeply embedded in the religious culture that people can hardly imagine any other form of leadership. Unfortunately, the Man of God syndrome has been exported to church leadership all over the world by Western TV ministries and traveling preachers.

Many years ago, in my endless quest to figure out how to reach multiple thousands, I visited one of the largest churches in America only to find that it had been seriously infected with the deadly MOGS. This huge church seemed to have all the contemporary earmarks of a successful modern mega-church: massive buildings, beautiful people, cool logo, state-of-the-art lighting and sound, and, of course, the ultimate common denominator of all über-churches—a larger-than-life superhero for a pastor. These superpastors often look more like supermodels with their toothpaste-commercial smiles, designer wardrobes, and styled hair.

But this guy took ministerial self-promotion to a whole new level. During his sermon I counted more than ten photos of himself on the four-page church bulletin. Or was it a souvenir program? I found myself playing "Where's Waldo?" or an "I Spy Pastor" game, circling his photos in my bulletin. Not only was he omnipresent on the printed page, the education building adjacent to the sanctuary bore his family name, as did the small wedding chapel. Isn't there a rule about waiting until a man is dead before sticking his name on coins and buildings? If not, maybe there should be.

"Are you trying to build
a ministry or
minister to My people?"

I thought about this experience recently after talking to a young campus minister about the difference between building a student ministry and ministering to students. Unfortunately, the Man of God syndrome that is epidemic in the church makes it quite common to build a "successful" ministry and at the same time do a lousy job of ministering to people. Programs and ministries are much easier to lead than people because programs are not sensitive, and they don't get offended when leaders act like self-absorbed jerks. On the other hand, people are extremely sensitive, and they do tend to get offended when not treated with respect.

BUILDING
A MINISTRY OR
MAKING DISCIPLES?

The more I thought about the idea (building a ministry or making disciples), the more the Holy Spirit seemed to aim pointed questions at me: "Are you more excited about finding new meeting places or meeting new people? Are you trying to build a ministry or minister to My people?"

Perhaps the real question I needed to ask myself was, Am I called to build a *ministry* or called to make *disciples?* Jesus calls all of His followers to make disciples, not to run a discipleship program. In order to make disciples, we must actually spend time with real live people, not just with Bible study books in Bible school classes, and not just in front of a TV camera or behind a desk.

Jesus never told His disciples to build churches or ministries for Him. He is quite capable of building His church in a way that the gates of hell will have serious problems. If we are trying to build His church, then we are trying to do something that only He can do. But if we do what He said to do—make disciples—then we will find that we are cooperating with Him. He will take those disciples and build His church. What a privilege to partner with the King of kings by simply ministering to people and empowering those people to minister to others.

I have no desire to be the "great man of God" or the "hero

preacher" with my name and face plastered all over everything. Does anyone really need a Steve Murrell International Ministries coffee mug? I am not even tempted in that direction because I am quite aware of the fact that I could never pull it off. I do not possess the charm, the money, the charisma or, most important, the desire.

I meet people all the time who, after spending a few minutes with me, have a kind of bewildered look on their faces. I am familiar with the look, and I usually know what they are thinking. They have heard about our numbers, our discipleship process, and the impact of Victory in the Philippines. Then they meet me, and they have a hard time connecting the dots. I definitely do not fit their "great man of God" leadership paradigm. I usually think to myself, "Sorry to disappoint you, but it's me, and what you see is what you get." If I have a passion with regard to leadership, it is that tens of thousands of young leaders will outshine, out-preach, and outperform me.

The apostle Paul seemed to be irritated with the fact that some in the Corinthian church were identifying themselves with him as their personal "man of God" rather than as simply followers of Christ. (See 1 Corinthians 3:3–5.) He fought the deadly MOGS virus that was creeping into the church. "I planted the seed, Apollos watered it, but God made it grow. So neither he who plants nor he who waters is anything, but only God, who makes things grow" (vv. 6–7). Throughout his letter to the Corinthians, as well as his other letters, Paul was simply saying, "It's not about me."

Timothy was a young leader who may have felt up to his neck, if not over his head, with all that Paul had empowered him to do. He was teaching, appointing elders, and moderating disputes among people much older than himself, all in a culture that honored age and ignored youth. Paul wrote to him saying:

> Don't let anyone look down on you because you are young, but set an example for the believers in speech, in life, in love, in faith and in purity.
>
> —1 Timothy 4:12

In his second letter to Timothy, Paul again wrote:

> The things you have heard me say in the presence of many witnesses entrust to reliable men who will also be qualified to teach others.
>
> —2 Timothy 2:2

There are four generations of leadership in that verse—Paul, Timothy, faithful men, and the others they would teach. You get the impression that very little time was allotted between generation one and generation four. Equipping and empowering was the modus operandi for Jesus and His apostles. It was just the way He did things. The task was too big, and the time too short, for anything else.

An Empowering Culture

Authority—how it is handled and understood—will either create an empowering environment or cripple our ability to turn disciples into leaders. Some of us have worked in an atmosphere in which everyone was encouraged to use his or her own ingenuity to try new ideas without the fear of failure. Some of us have also been in leadership environments that were so highly controlled that everyone was paralyzed with the fear of making a mistake.

The Victory leadership team has intentionally tried to create a culture where creativity and initiative are rewarded and mistakes are celebrated. We constantly encourage people to start small groups and experiment with different times, locations, and approaches. We also regularly encourage people to terminate those small groups. If a group is dead, we do not pretend it is alive. We simply pronounce it dead, do an autopsy, learn what we can, and move on to try something else.

We work pretty hard to create and maintain that kind of empowering environment. We try to make the leader with the longest losing streak feel like the great inventor Thomas Edison. Edison counted every failed attempt at inventing the electric light bulb as a great discovery of one more thing that would not work. I assure you, we have discovered a great many ways that small groups will not work.

When we talk about empowering people's creativity and ingenuity, it is assumed in our circles that we empower them to lead within the framework of our vision. We are not simply open to everything. Actually, we're not open to anything that falls outside the mission, vision, and values of Victory. What we equip and empower people to do is make disciples. People whose passion and calling do not contribute to those ends would be better served at a church capable of embracing and supporting their particular vision.

We also try to ensure that our conversation maintains that atmosphere of empowerment: "Maybe your small group is not working because of the time. Meeting at 4:00 a.m. was very innovative, but perhaps you should try something a little closer to sunrise." Or, "Maybe it's the venue, the target audience, or the content. I'm sure it's not you. You're great, and you're going to be very successful at this. Let's just try something else."

MISTAKES
ARE OK

I remember a conversation I had with L. A. Mumar, who was leading our campus ministry a few years ago. LA had a firm mental grasp on the empowering process at Victory, but in the face of some very difficult decisions, he was having a hard time applying it. Senior leaders at Victory are always available to counsel with next-generation leaders as they make tough leadership decisions. Over several conversations, however, I could sense LA hesitating, second-guessing himself, and trying to figure out what I would do in his situation.

My goal is not to delegate to others the responsibility of making the same decisions I would make, but to empower them as leaders to make decisions themselves. I made that clear by saying, "LA, I can live with you making wrong decisions, but I cannot live with you *not* making decisions." That one extra comment was all he needed. He handled the situation with great wisdom—maybe not the way I would have done it, but that was not the point. We can, if need be, fix problems caused by the shortsighted or uninformed decisions of young leaders, we can endure periods of slower growth as a result, or we can provide more support. What we cannot do, however, is raise up the next generation of leaders without creating and maintaining the atmosphere of empowerment.

Many visionary leaders are lightning-quick to come up with new ideas, new slogans, and new solutions. We definitely need those kinds of people on our team. They shake things up, rage against complacency, and keep the energy level high. Other leadership styles tend to focus more on process. That's me. Thankfully, we have both of those leadership types on the Victory team. When we are all working toward the same goal, the result is that we are never satisfied with the status quo. But we also understand that nothing is created perfectly on the first try, that it takes time to get it right.

We may get to version 5.0 before it really begins to bear fruit as we had expected. What we don't do is throw it all out every six months and start over with the latest get-big-quick church growth scheme. We allow the evolutionary process to do its thing and make our discipleship strategy better over time. We hold to the basics and constantly change the rest as needed.

Do not confuse simple with easy.

That is the way we have approached each part in our discipleship process—lots of mistakes, lots of trial and error, lots of evolving methodology and gradual improvement—while holding to the basics. We have been working on our equipping process for many years, and the more that process is developed, the more confident we are about empowering young disciples with greater responsibility.

Do not confuse simple with easy. The process of fasting, praying, engaging the community, and leading a small group requires dedication, compassion, and sacrifice. It is not at all easy, but it is not complicated either. As the process of equipping ("Training for Victory" class) and the process of engaging (leading small groups) have developed through the years, our confidence to empower new believers to be small group leaders has increased. Within the first year of following Christ, many are making disciples, establishing spiritual foundations, and equipping new disciples to make other disciples. In an earlier chapter I made reference to a quote about how systems enable ordinary people to do extraordinary things. At Victory we have a lot of ordinary people doing a lot of extraordinary things.

EQUIP
AND EMPOWER

The fourth part of the Victory discipleship process is to *empower disciples to make disciples.* In this chapter and the previous one, equipping and empowering are often mentioned in the same context. These two elements of our process are linked together like Siamese twins. They are both based on the simple belief that every disciple should make disciples and every believer should be a minister. That idea shapes everything we do to equip and train our Victory people with basic ministry skills.

A church's training usually follows the church's objectives.

Invert that equation and you get this: an inventory of a church's training will reveal a lot about the church's true purpose and intent. Some churches equip endlessly—providing classes, seminars, and online courses on every topic imaginable. All that training is good, except that the majority of a traditional church's training is geared toward Christian living, not Christian serving or Christian ministry. In other words, we teach people what to believe, how to confess their faith, how to be reconciled, how to raise their children, how to manage their finances, how to treat their spouses, how to exercise, how to pray, how to eat. The common denominator of those trainings is that every application relates to the believers and their own families. You can practice all that Christianity in the comfort of your own home. If, on the other hand, the church is committed to the Great Commission, to engaging culture, to establishing foundations, and to every member being a minister, it will radically affect the purpose and content of equipping.

Although the equipping and empowering elements of our discipleship process are similar, interrelated, and based on the same idea, it is important to understand that they are not the same thing. The easiest way to see the difference is to think about what happens when you take one of those elements away. What does it look like when a church is diligent to equip but does not empower people to minister? What if the church freely empowers people without them being well equipped? If we equip every member to minister, then we are also compelled to provide a platform for every person in our church to put those ministry skills into practice.

I have visited churches on the day when training school

graduates stand up on a stage to receive certificates for completing a course in ministry. Too often there is a sad but certain awareness that there is nothing for them to do—no clearly defined next step, no process or platform for them to begin putting their training into practice. Eventually many overequipped and under-empowered disciples will drop out, others will look for another church, and some will just settle into a role as spectators or critics. A few will be bold enough to empower themselves and create their own opportunities. Unfortunately, only a few will do this, and often they will find their opportunity in another ministry or in a new ministry they create for themselves. Sometimes the ministry they create will form a splinter group from the church where they were equipped but not empowered.

On the other hand, empowering people to take ministry responsibility without proper training and a well-established foundation can lead to all sorts of problems. The danger of empowering without proper equipping includes, of course, people teaching strange doctrines or making unwise ministry choices. But empowering without equipping is also unfair to the disciples because asking people to do things they are not equipped to do is simply setting them up to fail. Helping someone get over a series of ministry failures takes far more personal ministry and discipleship than training and equipping people to avoid the failures before ministry begins.

THE FOUR ES OF DISCIPLESHIP

In order to be effective, the discipleship process must be made up of several interrelated principles all working together, the objective being to make disciples. Those *principles* are:

1. *Engaging* culture and community

2. *Establishing* biblical foundations

3. *Equipping* believers to minister

4. *Empowering* disciples to make disciples

The key is that those principles must be *interrelated* and *all working together*. They are interrelated because we could not empower so many young believers unless we effectively established spiritual foundations and equipped them with basic ministry skills. Neither could we empower so many young believers unless new disciples could easily step into an ongoing process of engaging nonbelievers. We could not continue to engage nonbelievers if we were not effectively equipping and empowering new generations of disciples to make disciples.

Each of those principles also must *work together*. If you take away one of those elements—or just allow one to diminish in its effectiveness—the entire discipleship process breaks down. Each principle fuels the next and enables the previous.

WikiChurch Lessons

In a WikiChurch, you don't need to *find* a "great man or woman of God" and get a trickle-down anointing. You need to *be* a man or woman of God and realize that God has anointed you to do ministry and to make disciples. Once you have responded to the gospel, storm-proofed your life with strong biblical foundations, and gotten equipped with basic ministry skills, it is time to start making disciples by engaging your culture and your community. Whether you are young or old, a pastor or a plumber, male or female—*now* is the time for you to go and make disciples.

PRINCIPLE
Empower Believers
to Make Disciples

KEY VERSES
Matthew 28:19–20
2 Timothy 2:2

GOAL
Confidence and
Competence to
Make Disciples

CHAPTER NINE

LEADING WITH THE
NEXT GENERATION

WHILE RUMMAGING THROUGH my office last year, I found a tattered brown envelope filled with old photos from our original 1984 U-Belt outreach. Those old pictures brought back memories that had been buried under twenty-six years of activities. Looking at those photos and remembering the beginning, I was struck with a fresh realization of how very young we were then. I had hair back then, and the dedication and passion in our faces were palpable. We were in our early twenties, full of faith and vision, confident that God was about to do something big and we were right in the center of His plan. When I view those photos now that I'm in my fifties, Deborah and I look like school kids. It is a good thing we didn't see ourselves like that back then.

Some might have said that our team—a bunch of college students barely out of our teens—was naïve to believe we could slay such formidable giants. Those giants were the spiritual, cultural, financial, and even political obstacles that stood in the way of what we sensed God wanted to accomplish in the Philippines. There may have been some truth in those naysayers' claims. We were pretty naïve. On the other hand, big vision, unquenchable faith, and passion for others to know Christ come naturally to young believers. Doubt, fear, and hesitation are learned over time. It's a good thing we didn't have leaders anxious to point out how much we lacked in age, training, and experience. If the team of American students had not possessed a belief that all things were possible, nothing would have ever happened. In fact, we all would have been doing something else that summer.

THE RISKY BUSINESS OF EMPOWERING PEOPLE

Rice and I were a part of an organization that was willing to trust great responsibility to unproven young people— Maranatha Campus Ministries. Maranatha emerged out of the Jesus movement in the mid-1970s. Some of the group's older and more mature leaders were designated as elders, executive board members, pastors, and even apostles. When I say "older and more mature," I mean that most of those leaders were in their mid- to late-twenties, while the younger Maranatha members were mostly high school and college students.

The reputation was that Maranatha people were radical, committed, and willing to do anything for the cause of Christ.

Along with all the evangelizing, disciple making, and missionary sending, there naturally were mistakes that resulted from passionate but immature leadership. I have never met people with more passion and zeal to advance the kingdom of God than those Maranatha leaders. However, the way these immature and untrained leaders implemented that zeal on a local level was often ill advised. Thinking back on my college days, I remember what Joe Smith, one of the older Maranatha leaders, used to say: "We judge others by their actions, and we judge ourselves by the intentions of our hearts." That insight has stuck with me all these years and given me pause before criticizing what others are doing or have done.

> *I didn't have a clue what I was*
> *doing, but that didn't stop me.*

When I was a university student, I considered Joe a wise old sage. The shocking thing about that memory is that I am now much older than Joe was when I saw him as an old guy. Could Maranatha have benefited from older more mature leaders and a more balanced leadership structure? Absolutely! But what Maranatha did not need was a group of "seasoned leaders" who would keep young believers from stepping out with bold faith, taking risks for Christ, or being empowered with leadership responsibility.

I was still in college, having just turned twenty, when I

was designated a licensed minister and charged with leading a campus church with about forty college students. I didn't have a clue what I was doing, but that didn't stop me. I learned as I went, mostly by trial and lots of errors. It was quite amazing how after so many years, I still keep hearing about students from the campus ministry in Starkville, Mississippi, who are doing extraordinary things for Christ all over the world.

One of the benefits for Rice, me, and others in the Maranatha ministry in Starkville was the leader, Walter Walker. He emphasized faith, foundations, evangelism, discipleship, and unconditional surrender to Christ. He convinced us that all things were possible and that we could change the world. What he failed to point out was the limitation of our youth. But why should he, since Walter and his wife, Linda, were only a few years older than the rest of us?

Despite excellent leaders such as Walter, the problems within Maranatha Campus Ministries finally led to it being officially disbanded a few years after Deborah and I moved to the Philippines. Despite Maranatha's shortcomings, I am thankful to have been part of a ministry that unapologetically empowered next-generation leaders.

CROSSING THE FINISH LINE TOGETHER

Every church, denomination, and missionary organization faces the challenge of what to do with the next generation. How does the founding generation give the next generation the same opportunities it had? The same dynamics exist in secular nonprofits, corporations, and family businesses. They have to figure out how two culturally diverse generations can work and build together.

There seems to be two different approaches to this next-generation issue. The first is the traditional "pass the baton" relay race analogy. One generation has the baton and runs the race. The next does not have the baton, so it waits and watches. After the baton has changed hands, the first runner is no longer part of the race. This is why some old guys will never pass the baton until they are dead. They do not feel they have finished their race, so they hold the baton and guard it from the devil—and from the next generation. There has to be a better way.

One of my all-time favorite Olympic stories illustrates the better way. The scene was the 1988 Summer Olympics in Seoul, South Korea. Eight men were scheduled to start the 400-meter race, but British runner Derek Redmond had to withdraw at the last minute because of an injury to his Achilles tendon.[1] The pain in his heart was greater than the pain in his leg as he watched his fellow Olympians cross the finish line. Like countless young athletes, Derek had dreamed of Olympic gold. Unlike most, Derek actually had the talent to win it.

Stubbornly refusing to let a torn Achilles tendon rob him of his lifelong dream, the young runner set his sights on the 1992 Barcelona Games. Four more years of training. Four more years of hard work. Four more years of dreaming about the gold. By 1991 Derek was back to world-class speed, leading his team to an upset victory in the four-man 400-meter relay in the World Championships.[2] Another year and his Olympic dream could become reality.

At the 1992 Summer Olympics in Barcelona, Spain, Derek Redmond lined up with seven others in the 400-meter race. This time he was a heavy favorite not just to finish but to win a medal, possibly a gold. Derek's dad and number one fan, Jim Redmond, was among the sixty-five thousand spectators in the stands that day.

The starter fired his gun. Derek had one of the best starts of his career. Approaching the halfway mark, however, he heard a strange "pop." Disaster struck again. As he crashed to the track with a torn hamstring, seven men flew past him, racing for his medal. In a few seconds, the race was over. The cheering had stopped, and all eyes were on Derek Redmond, who had managed to peel himself off the track and, despite the pain, was slowly hobbling toward the finish line.

Suddenly a man broke past the security guards and leaped onto the track. He sprinted past the medics who had been trying in vain to get Derek to lie down on their stretcher. As the man caught up with the injured Olympian, the sprinter melted into his arms. After a brief conversation, Derek continued his struggle to finish the last fifty meters of the race—now with two strong arms and two healthy legs supporting him.

Just as they approached the finish line, the big man stepped back to allow Derek to cross on his own. Then he returned, and the men *exited the track together.* Derek set the record for the slowest 400-meter time in the history of the Olympics, but that didn't stop the sixty-five thousand fans from standing to their feet and giving the greatest applause of the whole 1992 Games. Who was the man, and what was that brief conversation all about? The man was Jim Redmond, Derek's dad. Here's how the conversation went.

"Look, son, you don't have to do this."

Despite the pain, Derek responded, "Yes, I do."

"Well, if you are going to finish this race, we'll finish it together." With those words, Jim helped his son finish the race.[3]

If we do not empower the next generation in some way now, we will lose them.

Discipleship and leadership are like a race—but not like a relay race where one generation passes the baton to the next and then retires to the locker room. Multigenerational discipleship and leadership are more like Derek Redmond and his dad—two generations crossing the finish line together.

In most older organizations, the next generation of leaders was expected to do their jobs, bide their time, and remember their place. Then one day it would be their turn to lead. This model stopped working years ago. The best young talent in a corporation is probably not going to sit patiently for ten to twenty years waiting his turn. If we do not empower the next generation in some way now, we will lose them. That's why we need to always look for, equip, and empower next-generation leaders.

Who's Next?

The Victory leadership team is constantly asking, "Where is the next generation of leaders?" We are not just looking for the next group of senior leaders in their forties and fifties; we seek to identify an emerging group of leaders in every age group and demographic. Sure, we have had visiting Christian leaders comment on the passion and maturity of our young leaders, but that doesn't necessarily mean we are *currently* doing a good job of discipling and training. It means only that we were doing a good job about *five years ago*. If we become complacent about leadership development and empowerment only to realize it after leaders stop emerging, then we will have woken up five years behind the problem. Momentum is a beautiful thing. It is much easier to keep something going than to restart the process after it has come to a stop.

One day I began thinking about multigenerational leadership, not necessarily biological generations but generations in terms of discipleship. As Paul wrote to Timothy, "The things you have heard me say in the presence of many witnesses entrust to reliable men who will also be qualified to teach others" (2 Tim. 2:2). I thought about some of the men I first began discipling twenty-seven years ago in the initial U-Belt outreach—Jun, Juray, Ferdie. A few years later another leadership generation emerged—Manny, Michael, Ariel, Julius, and others. Then the Rico, Robert, Mark, Gilbert, Paolo generation came on the scene.

On their heels was another generation—Dennis, LA, and their crowd. Then came another group of young leaders in their twenties with endless energy and crazy ideas—Joe,

Rich, Dan, Patrick, and others. New leaders are constantly emerging from our Kids' Church and youth groups who are already equipped, empowered, and experienced in making disciples. These upcoming leadership generations live on the cutting edge of cultural transitions and know more about engaging their particular generation than our senior leadership team ever will. They are smart, compassionate, and bold. And they are becoming world-class communicators.

When the Victory senior leadership team looks at those leadership generations, there are several inescapable realities. First of all, each group of leaders is far more knowledgeable, equipped, and experienced than any of us were at their age. Second, they are not like us. They think differently, problem-solve differently, and apply their faith to social needs in ways we never dreamed of as young leaders. Third, they are fully integrated and engaged with the culture. In many religious organizations leaders are likely to embrace a separation mentality and disconnect with the culture. To be effective, they have to relearn how to engage their communities.

That is not easy to do, and some are never able to genuinely reconnect, so they live in a strange irrelevant religious subculture. However, unlike their mentors, this new generation of leaders usually remains engaged with nonbelievers, so they never lose the ability to communicate and relate. Through the years we have become pretty effective at training new generations of disciples and leaders. We also have learned the importance of listening to younger leadership generations. However, those are actually the easy parts. The challenge for Victory and for every multigenerational organization is not just equipping and listening. It is learning how to empower and lead together with several leadership generations at the same time.

Leadership Lessons
From King Saul

We do not usually think of King Saul as a role model, except as an example of how we ought *not* to lead. But anyone can have a good day, even Saul. That was particularly true in his early years. There is at least one great leadership lesson we can learn from the first king of Israel.

Probably the best-known story of King Saul and young David was a conflict with the Philistine army and their champion, Goliath. The two armies were faced off, each encamped on hills separated by a valley. Each day the armies would assemble and form opposing battle lines. And each day the nine-foot-tall Philistine would step forward from the Philistine lines and challenge the army of Israel to send out their greatest warrior for a winner-take-all contest.

It is worth noting that the challenge was not just to the army of Israel in general but to its leader, King Saul. Saul had become king, in part, by virtue of being a skilled warrior and because of his height. He was head and shoulders taller than any other man in the kingdom (1 Sam. 9:2). Saul would have been the obvious choice to contend with Goliath, a fact that had probably occurred to every soldier in the army of Israel.

But day after day for forty days the armies lined up. Goliath stepped forward, issued the challenge, and taunted the armies of Israel. Each day the giant called them names and insulted them in every way imaginable in order to provoke them. But there was no response. The situation was both terrifying and embarrassing.

David remained at home with the lowly job of tending sheep while his three oldest brothers went off to become heroes in Saul's army. David periodically visited the battle lines to bring provisions to his brothers. On one of those visits David heard the insults and the challenge of Goliath.

Young David, full of faith, vision, and passion, was ready to fight and began inquiring about how he could be empowered to go out as Israel's representative. And, as is typical of the oldest brother, Eliab proceeded to put David back in his place.

> When Eliab, David's oldest brother, heard him speaking with the men, he burned with anger at him and asked, "Why have you come down here? And with whom did you leave those few sheep in the desert? I know how conceited you are and how wicked your heart is; you came down only to watch the battle."
>
> —1 SAMUEL 17:28

In Jesse's family, David was at the bottom of the pecking order. When the oldest of twelve brothers tells the youngest to get lost, that is usually the end of it. That is true today, but even more so in those days. In his older brothers' eyes, David was a rebellious little brat who was so full of himself that he would not take no for an answer. Eventually David made his way to Saul and persuaded Saul to let him go out and fight the Philistine. I never could understand why Saul would agree to such an outrageous proposal. After all, everything was at stake. Who knows what Saul saw in David. I would be willing to bet, however, that if David had volunteered on day three, he may never have gotten close to King Saul. Forty days of insults and intimidation had worn the king down.

To King Saul's credit, he went beyond his initial reservation about empowering such a young person to represent the nation. And, of course, he wanted to help David in any way that he could.

> Then Saul dressed David in his own tunic. He put a coat of armor on him and a bronze helmet on his head. David fastened on his sword over the tunic and tried walking around, because he was not used to them. "I cannot go in these," he said to Saul, "because I am not used to them." So he took them off. Then he took his staff in his hand, chose five smooth stones from the stream, put them in the pouch of his shepherd's bag and, with his sling in his hand, approached the Philistine.
>
> —1 Samuel 17:38–40

Also to Saul's credit, he not only overcame the tendency to discount David because of his youth, but the king also understood that if he was going to let the kid fight the battle none of the older soldiers were willing or able to fight, he would have to let David do it his way. Many emerging leaders today are like David was in his day. They are ready to fight, ready to engage in the battle of ideas where the church and its leadership are being taunted and challenged. Like David, they are not comfortable with Saul's armor, that is, the methods and approaches of previous leadership generations. Those previous leaders, like Saul, were once great warriors who fought and prevailed in their own battles. But they are no longer capable of confronting the cultural challenges of the present day.

Unfortunately, many organizations do not have young leaders equipped to engage these new cultural giants. Others have the potential young champions, but they insist on using old and outdated methods. They cannot bring themselves to empower young leaders and let them fight the battles their way.

You know how the story ends. David took five smooth stones and a slingshot and went out to confront Goliath. One stone hit Goliath in the forehead, the giant went down, and before the Philistines could respond, David was standing there holding up Goliath's severed head.

UNITING GENERATIONS

When movements have zealous but immature leadership structures, the movements often self-destruct. The redeeming value of an exploding movement is that young leaders are spun out in many directions, each finding a new place to serve. Go to any growing, dynamic Christian organization today, and you will find senior leaders who were saved and discipled in high-commitment evangelistic youth ministries. Often those leaders found their way to their current organizations because of leadership problems in the ministries where their faith, vision, and passion were developed. I call this a "redeeming value" because good came out of these movements even though they could have made a far greater impact for Christ if the leadership had been mature.

On the other hand, movements that do not effectively

equip and empower succeeding generations of leaders do not typically blow apart; they simply become irrelevant and ineffective in engaging the ever-changing culture. As a consequence, they eventually die off. The point is that we cannot surrender the church to the newest generation of leaders, nor can we simply put them in their place to wait for the current leaders to retire or die. The challenge for Victory and for every multigenerational organization is to learn how to lead together with the next generation.

Learn how to lead together
with the next generation.

We have been working on that idea for quite a while. It is a natural consequence of our processes of equipping and empowering. We have learned many things about how to do this and are learning more all the time. Listed below are what you might consider our top five lessons learned.

1. Security—Established leaders must be secure when young leaders start getting credit.

This was hardly the case with Saul.

> When the men were returning home after David had killed the Philistine, the women came out from all the towns of Israel to meet King Saul with singing and dancing, with joyful songs and with tambourines and lutes. As they danced, they sang: "Saul has slain his thousands, and David his tens of

thousands." Saul was very angry; this refrain galled him. "They have credited David with tens of thousands," he thought, "but me with only thousands. What more can he get but the kingdom?"

—1 Samuel 18:6–8

When David's congregation becomes bigger than yours, when the guy you discipled in your little group starts his own small groups and experiences explosive growth, it will test how secure you really are. Almost every time I have empowered younger guys to take over my responsibilities, they have quickly exceeded what I had been doing. As president of Every Nation Churches, I have responsibilities that frequently take me out of the country. Yet Victory grows as much or more in my absence than when I am at home. As a senior leader I have had to get over any insecurity about younger pastors taking it to the next level.

Insecurity in leadership is a deadly thing that will destroy any organization. It drives pastors and presidents to defensive positions, protecting their authority or exercising it simply to show who is the boss. Insecure leaders view subordinates with suspicion and jealousy. Insubordination is dealt with harshly. Empowering is based on strict obedience to the boss's wishes rather than creativity, ingenuity, and independent thinking.

That is an extreme picture of dysfunctional leadership. As we at Victory have tried to learn how to lead with the next generation, we have come to understand that the character of our leadership at every level must be more than simply the absence of that Saul-like insecurity; it must be Christlike. Paul wrote to the Philippian church about the character of Christ and how loosely Christ grasped His position.

> Your attitude should be the same as that of Christ
> Jesus: Who, being in very nature God, did not con-
> sider equality with God something to be grasped,
> but made himself nothing, taking the very nature
> of a servant...
>
> —Philippians 2:5–7

Insecurity in emerging leaders can have an equally cor-
rosive effect on an organization. Grasping for titles, position, and recognition; looking for ways to get a leg up on the
other emerging leaders—all of it works against an organization's ability to move forward with shared leadership among
multiple generations. Everyone has to follow the example of
Christ, but it is senior leaders from the top down who set the
standard for others to follow.

2. Respect—Established leaders must make room around the table for emerging leaders.

I was meeting with a group of North American campus
ministers a few years ago to discuss some leadership and control issues. One of the campus leaders vividly explained his
feelings with a familiar illustration of a family gathering.
He described the typical American Thanksgiving holiday.
Although Thanksgiving began in the United States as a feast
to thank God for a successful harvest, in modern times it has
become a national day of gluttony and professional football
games.

Usually relatives gather together for dinner with a table
for the adults and a kiddie table off in another room for all
the children. After painting a clear picture of the scene, the
campus minister said, "Steve, people talk about the importance

of the campuses, and we have responded to that call. But are we ever going to get to come in and sit at the adult table? When do campus ministers graduate from the kids' table?"

Established leaders need to make room at the big table for emerging leaders and not just give them spectator seats. We have to empower multigenerational leadership. I understand that the table is only so big, and making room for one could mean less room for another. Promotion and position at Victory are not based on age, time served, or even maturity. We focus on empowering the youngest leaders we can.

My former campus pastor, Walter Walker, came to Manila for Victory's twenty-fifth anniversary so he could better understand our discipleship culture and leadership philosophy. He asked several Victory pastors, "Would it surprise you if in the next ten years your immediate supervisor were someone in their twenties or thirties?" To his great surprise—and to mine—almost everyone said that they not only expected it but also welcomed it. I guess that's the result of creating an empowering culture that values and believes in the next generation.

David tried on Saul's armor and found that it did not work well with his approach to killing lions, bears, and Philistine giants. David simply said to Saul, "I cannot go in these...because I am not used to them" (1 Sam. 17:39). Instead of that simple response, what if David had complained to those fitting him with Saul's armor, "This old armor is a piece of junk! No wonder Saul and his army are so fearful and powerless. What a bunch of losers! I'll show 'em how it's done."

That is, of course, using a lot of imagination, but the reason I can see that happening is because I have seen exactly that attitude in a new wave of young leaders across the body of Christ. They seem to be almost angry or offended with the Christian leaders and institutions that existed before them. In fact, they define their ministry and their movement as a revolution against previous generations of leaders (Saul) and their methods (Saul's armor). Their goal is not to lead *with* the previous generation but to lead *without* them.

A word of advice to emerging leaders: If the armor doesn't fit, don't feel compelled to use it, but decline respectfully. To sit at the big table as part of a team that leads with the next generation, you must be respectful of that table. It did not just appear out of nowhere. Somebody had to sacrifice, believe God, and persevere to create it.

3. Humility—Established leaders must continue changing and improving the disciple-making process.

The methods and processes created for one generation will probably not continue to work in rapidly changing cultures unless there are constant adjustments. No matter how great or fruitful a discipleship system becomes, it has a limited shelf life. Senior leaders are naïve to think they can continue to engage succeeding generations of nonbelievers without having equipped and empowered twentysomethings and giving them meaningful seats around the table with them. Acknowledging the diminishing effectiveness of previous methods as well as the need for young leadership requires a measure of humility among the leadership team. Humility is the ticket to leadership for all participants—old, young, and in between.

As we know, Saul became intensely jealous of David, even though Saul knew that David had been chosen by God to succeed (or perhaps to replace) him. It seems strange that Saul would have been so jealous of such a loyal young man. Saul threw spears, conspired to have David killed, and personally hunted David after he fled for his life. Young David could never understand why Saul hated him so much. He had done nothing to betray the king and even refused to strike back when presented with the perfect opportunity. David would not so much as speak an unkind word against Saul. What possibly could have created such hostility?

Oh, yeah, that song. "Saul has slain his thousands, and David his tens of thousands" (1 Sam. 18:7). In reality, David had not slain tens of thousands, just one big Philistine and with a slingshot, no less. Notwithstanding the providence of God, some might have called it a lucky shot. However, the exaggerated body count made for a good story and a great song. It must have been a big hit, one of those tunes you just cannot get out of your head. As the song became famous, so did David. The Book of 1 Samuel mentions two instances when people who had never met David knew of him because of the song. (See 1 Samuel 21:11; 29:5.)

David didn't write the song and probably didn't do anything to promote it. But who among us would not have enjoyed hearing a hit song about some great thing he or she had done? That little tune must have driven Saul mad with jealousy. Samuel wrote, "Saul was very angry; this refrain galled him. 'They have credited David with tens of thousands,' he thought, 'but me with only thousands. What more can he get but the kingdom?' And from that time on Saul kept a jealous eye on David" (1 Sam. 18:8–9).

Young leaders need to be very careful about exaggerating the impact of their ministries.

A song. It is the only thing we read in the story of David and Saul that could have accounted for the king's insane jealousy. Although David had nothing to do with writing the song or its popularity, it destroyed his relationship with the king and his seat at the king's table. Young leaders need to be very careful about exaggerating the impact of their ministries and equally careful about allowing others to do it.

4. Unity—Established leaders must build a multigenerational team that is deeply committed to a common vision.

By God's grace, Victory has grown from 165 Filipino students to more than 52,000. And, by God's grace, we have never had to endure the pain of church splits and splinter groups. That doesn't mean it cannot happen. It doesn't mean that Victory leaders and Victory members are unlike any other church leaders or members. We have to fight the same battles, sidestep the same pitfalls, and resist the same temptations. I am also fully aware that there are hundreds of leaders at Victory–Manila who could quickly build their own ministries and become founders and senior pastors.

They would have no more Victory policies, no more waiting for their turn to preach, no more laboring in obscurity. Amazingly, though, they seem to prefer sticking around and building together. What makes that happen? There are probably more reasons than I am aware of, but at the very least, it comes from a common commitment to a big vision, equipping and empowering, giving young leaders meaningful seats at the table, and being willing to lead together with the next generation.

5. Trust—Established leaders must learn how to trust the next generation.

Some of the greatest lessons we can learn from people are the unintentional ones. These are the moments when no one is trying to make a big point or teach anything, but a transfer of knowledge just happens. This happened to me at a surprise birthday party. I was turning forty, and as is typical of that particular event, I expected endless jokes about my advanced age. Those expectations were fully met and exceeded.

Any and every funny or embarrassing moment of my life was recounted by people from church, individuals I had discipled, neighbors, staff, and even my own family. After about an hour, when it seemed to all that I had been sufficiently roasted, it was time to add a few kind words to honor me for my fifteen years of service at Victory. That is when I learned a great lesson.

To my surprise, there was almost nothing said about how well I had performed in the many challenging aspects of being a senior pastor. The list of demanding responsibilities that have burned out many a pastor is fairly long. You would think something would have been said about how hard I had worked to effectively accomplish those challenging tasks. But nobody complimented my inspiring sermons; nobody talked about my discipleship groups. Nothing was said about the

Bible study materials I had written; there were no comments on my great wisdom or leadership.

Joey Bonifacio was the first to say anything serious. A successful businessman and my next-door neighbor for twelve years, Joey had an obvious leadership and communication gift but was initially hesitant to become a church elder and later a pastor. Joey stood to speak and with no shortage of tears began to talk about how I had believed in him and entrusted huge ministry responsibilities to him when he had so little confidence in himself.

Manny Carlos picked up where Joey left off. Manny surrendered his life to Christ while earning his master's degree in business at the University of Virginia. He returned to the Philippines as a young Citibank manager on a fast track to power and prestige. Manny began talking about his lack of confidence to minister to others. He could not believe that I trusted him to be a pastor. According to Manny, it changed his life forever. Today Manny serves as the president of Victory's legal board and executive director of the Victory Ministers Association, and he recently was recognized as one of the few Philippine evangelical bishops by leaders in the body of Christ outside of Victory.

Then came Jun Escosar and Ferdie Cabiling, both original church members from 1984. Today Jun Escosar has earned a doctorate in missiology and is recognized as a leading missiologist specializing in church planting in Asia. Ferdie is known as an expert in discipleship and leadership development, having earned respect in the Philippines and in the church world abroad. Each one basically said, "I can't believe Steve trusted me to be a minister."

This went on for about an hour, with one leader after another telling their story of being entrusted and empowered with responsibilities that required a measure of confidence far beyond what they seemed to have on hand. Though almost each one was saying the same thing, there was nothing scripted about their comments. They were spontaneous and offered up with tearful sincerity.

Since the big party I have heard other young leaders make similar comments. They repeatedly say, "I can't believe they trusted me to..." Their remarks, however, were not directed to me but to other Victory leaders who had entrusted them with ministry responsibilities. I think Joey Bonifacio's initial comment at the party struck something very deep in people's hearts and experience. Over time the habit of entrusting and empowering young disciples to step into active ministry roles gradually became a part of Victory's organizational culture. Consequently, we had done a lot more to encourage next-generation leaders than we realized.

My fortieth surprise birthday had a great impact on the way I think about discipleship and leadership. It's really not that complicated—equip every disciple to minister; empower disciples to make disciples; then get out of the way. But as simple as that sounds, it is not always easy, especially if you are a control freak needing to keep a tight rein on everything around you. Many leaders are perfectionists who demand that everything be done their way. The result is that next-generation leaders are paralyzed and terrified they might make a mistake.

> *Empower disciples*
> *to make disciples; then*
> *get out of the way.*

That is the opposite of empowerment. It was certainly gratifying to be honored with such a display of emotion and appreciation at my birthday party. But lest I am tempted to get drunk on praise, I have to remind myself of exactly what they were saying. I was being honored for the great number of things that I did *not* do. In other words, everyone was expressing thanks to me for getting out of the way—and, particularly, out of *their* way. What all my tearful admirers did not know was that my trust in them was not nearly as great as they had imagined. What or, rather, whom I was really trusting was the Holy Spirit to enable them to do great things. And, I must say, I was also trusting the Holy Spirit to keep them from doing something crazy. Today I would trust any one of them with my life.

Many things have been said about using faith to accomplish great things. In the context of church leadership, one of the greatest and most important applications of faith is to trust the Holy Spirit to work in and through those you are leading. Without confidence that the Holy Spirit is in control, there is no empowering, no shared leadership, and, as a consequence, no multiplication.

WIKICHURCH LESSONS

A WikiChurch is a multigenerational church. Attempting to lead the next generation is common and safe. Attempting to lead *with* the next generation is rare and risky. Multigenerational leadership is difficult but achievable as long as we are willing to extend trust and respect.

It is probably easier to pass the baton to the next generation than it is to cross the finish line together because passing the baton does not require unity. Leading with the next generation requires us to think, relate, and build multigenerationally. It is a tough challenge, but it is worth the effort.

CHAPTER TEN

MAKING DISCIPLES,
DISCIPLING NATIONS

S OMETIMES POLITICS IN the Philippines feels like a strange combination of barrio, fiesta, and gang warfare. In the 2004 national election, sixteen Victory members ran for office. Fourteen won. As a result, we have church members who are senators, congressmen, mayors, governors, and city councilors. Their membership at Victory–Manila or one of the Victory churches in the provinces is not a result of some outreach to politicians but because we make disciples. Some of those disciples have felt called by God to run for office.

Don't get me wrong here: our church does not get involved in partisan politics. The Victory people who ran for office represented almost every political party in the nation. Victory is not for one party and against the others. Victory exists simply to honor God and make disciples, not to get people elected to office.

I do believe, however, the inevitable fruit of making disciples is that eventually those disciples will impact their culture and their community. In other words, they will disciple nations.

The modern evangelical church tends to celebrate the Great Commission to disciple *individuals* while ignoring the cultural mandate to disciple nations. One reason for the neglect is our gross ignorance of history. We know all about preachers and missionaries who evangelized pagan souls, but we know little about reformers and educators who helped transform pagan nations. We celebrate and honor soul-winning preachers such as John Wesley and George Whitefield. However, we forget about nation-changing, disciple-making Christian statesmen such as William Wilberforce and John Witherspoon.

Because of our short-term mentality, the separation of church and state doctrine, and our Western evangelical obsession with the individual, we have missed the point of the Matthew 28 commission: "All authority in heaven and on earth has been given to me. Therefore go and make disciples *of all nations*" (Matt. 28:18–19, emphasis added).

We make disciples, but we rarely disciple nations. We reach out to unreached people groups, but we flee from ungodly culture. We expect moral change but not social change. Shouldn't disciples have a positive impact on their communities? Is it actually possible to disciple a nation? Can the gospel really change society, or should we expect everything to get worse and worse until Armageddon? Is our ultimate goal simply not to be left behind after the Rapture? Is there a valid hope to influence nations for the glory of God? A quick look at history tells us that, yes, the gospel really can and should influence nations.

THE MAN WHO SAVED WESTERN CIVILIZATION

Fifteen hundred years ago Ireland was an idol-worshiping, slave-trading nation of savage pagans. In just one generation Ireland was transformed into a godly nation known for its scholars and missionaries. In his best-selling book *How the Irish Saved Civilization,* Thomas Cahill writes that this national transformation was primarily the work of one man— Patrick.

When Patrick was a teenager in Britain, he was captured by pirates and forced into slavery in Ireland. During this time he had a life-changing encounter with the Lord. After six years of cruel slavery, he escaped and returned home, but he soon received a divine call to return to minister to those who had enslaved him. In a vision, he heard one of his captors say, "We beg you to come and walk among us once more."[1] Can you imagine being called to minister the love of Jesus to the very people who had enslaved you for six years? Patrick responded to that vision and returned to Ireland to preach the gospel.

Shouldn't disciples have a positive
impact on their communities? Is it
actually possible to disciple a nation?

During his thirty years of missionary work in Ireland, Patrick helped establish more than seven hundred churches and schools and trained more than three thousand ministers, many of whom went as missionaries to Scotland, England, France, Switzerland, Germany, and Italy. Patrick's schools became some of the most important learning institutions in Europe during the Middle Ages, but his ministry went beyond just church work. He also helped transform government and reform laws that brought the end of slavery in Ireland.[2]

THE MAN WHO
ENDED THE SLAVE TRADE

It took another man of God to end the slave trade in Britain. Raised in a family with wealth and status, William Wilberforce was elected to the British Parliament at the age of twenty-one. Five years later he read *The Rise and Progress of Religion in the Soul* and surrendered his life fully to Christ. He immediately felt an overwhelming burden to share the gospel with everyone he met and wondered if he should quit Parliament and enter full-time ministry. John Newton, his mentor and a repentant former slave owner, convinced him to remain in Parliament and take up the fight to end the slave trade in the British Empire.[3]

His renewed sense of divine calling produced a twofold life mission, as indicated in his diary entry on October 28, 1787: "God Almighty has set before me two great objects; the suppression of the slave trade and the reformation of manners."[4]

Convinced that God wanted him to stay in government to fight slavery, Wilberforce introduced a bill in the House of Commons in 1789 to abolish the English slave trade. It was defeated, but Wilberforce was not. He reintroduced the bill every year for the next eighteen years until it was finally passed in 1807, ending the English slave trade.[5] But that was not the end of his work. He then set his sights on not merely abolishing the slave trade in England but also on ending slavery in the British Empire. He worked tirelessly to change English law, English culture, and the English economy in order to end the British slave trade. Finally in 1833, forty-five years after Wilberforce started his fight to end slavery, the bill that would abolish all slavery in the British Empire was passed. Wilberforce died a few days later, and more than eight hundred thousand slaves were freed.[6]

This was not done by a preacher but by a Christian serving God in civil government.

THE MAN WHO
SHAPED THE MEN
WHO SHAPED AMERICA

In 1768 John Witherspoon resigned his pastorate in Scotland and moved to the New World to pursue a career in education. Some might say he walked away from his calling, but in reality he had not abandoned his faith or his calling. He served God as an educator the same way he had served God as a pastor. He became the president of a school that trained ministers, the College of New Jersey (now the apostate Princeton University).

Many of Witherspoon's graduates became pastors and ministers. Those who did not end up in ministry became leaders in other fields. His graduates include a US president, a US vice president, ten cabinet officials, twenty-one senators, thirty-nine congressmen, one Supreme Court justice, one-fifth of the signers of the US Declaration of Independence, and one-sixth of the delegates to the US Constitutional Convention.[7] Witherspoon is called "the man who shaped the men who shaped America." In other words, Witherspoon discipled a nation.

Where are the modern versions of Patrick, Wilberforce, and Witherspoon who will right social wrongs and change unjust laws, who will serve in government and build God-honoring educational institutions? Unfortunately, most Christians are too busy with prayer meetings and Bible studies to effectively engage their cultures and disciple their nations. Real Christianity is not measured by how much time we spend in church but by how we apply God's Word in all of life. Let's applaud and support every godly citizen who is willing to obey the Great Commission by not just discipling individuals but by applying their faith to all of life.

WIKICHURCH LESSONS

WikiChurches not only make disciples, but they also disciple nations. Jesus told His original disciples to "go and make disciples of all nations" (Matt. 28:19). The starting point of discipling nations is discipling individuals, families, clans, and communities. As we *engage* our communities, *establish* biblical foundations, *equip* believers to minister, and *empower* them to make disciples, it is only a matter of time before whole communities, cities, and nations will be impacted for the honor and glory of God.

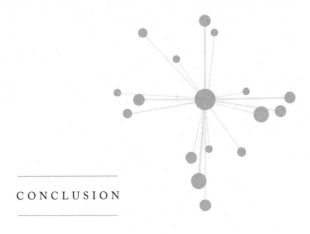

HIS LAST COMMAND,
OUR FIRST PRIORITY

I T WAS A small gathering with a big name—the World Apostolic Summit. February 1999. Singapore. The Y2K frenzy was hitting warp speed. Was this to be the end of life as we knew it and the beginning of some catastrophic digital apocalypse? To figure it all out, thirty "apostles" from around the world spent three days answering the question, "What do you feel God is saying to His church?"

As usual, I was the youngest minister in the room and the only one wearing jeans. I was also the only one who was not formally asked to this invitation-only gathering. I was a last-minute substitute for my friend Rice Broocks.

Listening to these spiritual giants talk about what God

was doing in their nations, I was simultaneously inspired and intimidated. I felt like a lion in a den of Daniels. When it was finally my turn to suggest what I felt the Lord was saying to His church in 1999, I said that I thought He was saying the same thing he said in 1899, in 1599, in 999, and in 99: "Go and make disciples." As it turned out, I was the only one in the room who mentioned anything about making disciples.

EVERYTHING BUT DISCIPLESHIP

Why do church leaders spend time and energy doing everything but making disciples? Why do we try every church-growth gimmick known to mankind yet ignore the one strategy Jesus endorsed? Shouldn't His last message be our first option?

For Jesus, discipleship was and still is top priority. Yes, He fed the hungry and healed the sick. But He always gave the twelve disciples His prime time. His final word to them before He ascended into heaven was a commission not just to be disciples, but also to *make* disciples. Like the original followers of Jesus, we are supposed to be disciples, and we are supposed to *make* disciples. In other words, we are supposed to follow Jesus, and we are supposed to help others follow Him.

Shouldn't Jesus's last message
be our first option?

SIMPLE STEPS FOR
CAVEMEN AND FISHERMEN

Discipleship isn't supposed to be complicated. Difficult, yes. Complicated, no. Two thousand years ago discipleship was so simple that a carpenter explained it to uneducated fishermen in one sentence: "Follow me, and I will show you how to fish for people!" (Matt. 4:19, NLT). Those simple fishermen followed, fished, and changed their world.

If modern discipleship is confusing or complicated, it is because we have strayed from biblical principles and the simple biblical process that Jesus lived and taught His disciples. Sadly, the fruit of this departure is glaringly evident today in the church. I have read discipleship books and manuals that were so confusing they made quantum physics seem simple. You would have had to be a rocket scientist or a brain surgeon to figure it out.

I loved the GEICO insurance commercials that used cavemen to promote the idea that using their website is "so easy, a caveman can do it." The book you just read is my attempt to present a simple step-by-step discipleship process more for the caveman than the rocket scientist. The principles that created this simple process are universal and timeless. They worked for us in Manila, and I believe they will work for you anywhere in the world.

Whether you are a veteran disciple and disciple-maker or a new believer, I hope this book has provoked and inspired you to be a disciple and to make disciples with greater intentionality. As you engage, establish, equip, and empower the next generation of disciples, remember these five thoughts.

1. Follow principles, not models.

Don't take the easy route and copy a model that seems to be working somewhere else. Do the hard work of discovering principles and applying them in your own culture and in your own community. A model that works somewhere else probably will not work for you, but principles are universal and timeless. Discover them, and they will work for you.

2. Focus on process, not events.

Disciple-making is a process that systematically moves people toward Christ and spiritual maturity; it is not a bunch of randomly disconnected church activities such as foundation class, membership class, discipleship class, Bible school, leadership class, or ministries for men, women, and youth. Ministry activities, events, and departments are much more effective when they are integrated into a strategic discipleship process. Disconnected, stand-alone events, ministries, and meetings often compete with the real priority—making disciples.

3. Develop a culture, not methods.

Disciple-making churches are fueled by a discipleship culture, not by a magic "silver bullet" method. When the culture is right, almost any method will work. When the culture is toxic, even the best method will fail. Here's the challenge: changing methods is quick and easy (some leaders change methods monthly), but changing culture is hard work and takes years. Do the hard work and build a discipleship culture; don't just import a discipleship method.

4. Concentrate on consistency, not creativity.

Creativity is way overrated. When it comes to making disciples, I have found that if we keep on doing the "same ole boring strokes" long enough, they will eventually bear fruit. Most people quit or change too soon. Just when the old *Good to Great* flywheel is about to start spinning, we trade it for the latest, greatest creative idea. Consistency is always more powerful than the elusive and creative "silver bullet" solution of the month.

5. Build relationships, not programs.

I agree with my good friend Joey Bonifacio, who always says, "Discipleship is relationship." There are three levels of relationship that must be developed in the discipleship process: relationship with Jesus, relationship with unbelievers, and relationship with believers. The more we celebrate all three relationships, the more we will build a healthy discipleship culture. Discipleship is relationship.

So what is God saying to His people today? I believe He's saying the same thing He said one hundred years ago, two hundred years ago, and two thousand years ago to His followers in Jerusalem: "Go and make disciples of all nations."

Remember, this was a carpenter talking to uneducated fishermen. He was not a brain surgeon talking to rocket scientists. Discipleship is so simple we all can do it—whether male, female, young, old, rich, or poor. We just need to practice the *same ole boring strokes*!

NOTES

INTRODUCTION
WHAT IS A WIKICHURCH?

1. Wikipedia.com, "Nupedia," http://en.wikipedia.org/wiki/Nupedia (accessed February 17, 2011).

2. Wikipedia.com, "History of Wikipedia," http://en.wikipedia.org/wiki/History_of_Wikipedia (accessed February 17, 2011).

3. Jim Gills, "Special Report: Internet Encyclopaedias Go Head to Head," December 15, 2005, *Nature* 438 (December 15, 2005): 900–904, abstract viewed at http://www.nature.com/nature/journal/v438/n7070/full/438900a.html (accessed February 17, 2011); Roy Rosenzweig, "Can History Be Open Source? *Wikipedia* and the Future of the Past," *Journal of American History* 93, no. 1 (June 2006): 117–146.

4. TheOfficeQuotes.com, "*The Office* Season 3 Quotes," http://www.theofficequotes.com/season-3/the-negotiation (accessed February 17, 2011).

CHAPTER 2
ONE-ARMED JUDO

1. Michael E. Gerber, *The E-Myth Revisited: Why Most Small Businesses Don't Work and What to Do About It*, 3rd edition (New York: HarperCollins, 1995), 101.

CHAPTER 3
HITTING THE WRONG TARGET

1. Steve Rivera, "Emmons Loses Gold Medal After Aiming at Wrong Target," *USA Today*, August 22, 2004, http://www.usatoday.com/sports/olympics/athens/skill/2004 -08-22-shooting-emmons_x.htm (accessed February 8, 2011).

2. Rick Warren, interview by David Chrzan, "The Importance of Evangelism for Church Growth," Rick Warren's Ministry Podcast, podcast audio, June 14, 2007, http://itunes.apple.com/us/podcast/rick-warrens-ministry -podcast/id251173470 (accessed April 15, 2011).

3. Jen Brown, "The Romance Behind Games' First Gold," MSNBC.com, August 10, 2008, http://today.msnbc.msn .com/id/26124639/ns/today-today_in_beijing/ (accessed March 16, 2011).

CHAPTER 4
THE POWER OF PROCESS

1. John Wesley Etheridge, *The Life of the Rev. Adam Clarke*, 2nd edition (London: John Mason, 14, City-Road, 1858), 165–166.

2. Ibid., 166.

CHAPTER 5
CATCHING BIRDS, FISHING FOR MEN, AND ASHTRAY EVANGELISM

1. Jonathan Eig, *Opening Day: The Story of Jackie Robinson's First Season* (New York: Simon & Schuster, 2008), 127.

2. Ibid.

3. Jackie Robinson, *I Never Had It Made: An Autobiography of Jackie Robinson* (New York: Harper Perennial, 2003), 63–64.

4. Chuck Quinley, *I Want to Bear Fruit* (Doraville, GA: USA Church Strengthening Ministry, Inc, 2000), 110.

5. Ibid.

CHAPTER 6
GOOD FAÇADE, BAD FOUNDATIONS

1. Jerry Camarillo Dunn Jr., "The Leaning Tower of Pisa," HowStuffWorks.com, http://adventure.howstuffworks.com/leaning-tower-of-pisa-landmark.htm (accessed February 9, 2011); TowerofPisa.info, "Tower of Pisa History," http://www.towerofpisa.info/Tower-of-Pisa-history.html (accessed February 17, 2011).

2. TowerofPisa.info, "Tower of Pisa History."

3. Ibid.

4. Ibid.

5. Dunn Jr., "The Leaning Tower of Pisa."

6. Randy Alfred, "December 15, 2001: Leaning Tower of Pisa Reopens With New Angle," Wired.com, December 15, 2001, http://www.wired.com/thisdayintech/2010/12/1215 leaning-tower-pisa-reopens (accessed February 17, 2011).

7. *New York Times*, "Earthquake in the Philippines Kills at Least 258, Including 48 Children in One School," July 17, 1990, http://www.nytimes.com/1990/07/17/world/earthquake -philippines-kills-least-258-including-48-children-one-school .html (accessed February 9, 2011).

8. Centers for Disease Control and Prevention, "International Notes Earthquake Disaster—Luzon, Philippines," *MMWR Weekly* 39, no. 34 (August 31, 1990): 573–577, http://www.cdc.gov/mmwr/preview/ mmwrhtml/00001734.htm (accessed February 9, 2011).

CHAPTER 9
LEADING WITH
THE NEXT GENERATION

1. Rick Weinberg, "94: Derek and Dad Finish Olympic 400 Together," ESPN.com, http://sports.espn.go.com/espn/ espn25/story?page=moments/94 (accessed February 16, 2011).

2. DerekRedmond.com, "Profile," http://www .derekredmond.com/profile.asp (accessed February 16, 2011).

3. Weinberg, "94: Derek and Dad Finish Olympic 400 Together."